MATAWAN AND ABERDEEN

OF TOWN AND FIELD

Matawan was home to several bakeries over the years, including C. Gelhaus, J. Gesler (seen in this glass lantern slide from the 1800s), and the Matawan Bakery on 143 Main Street. Both Gesler and Gelhaus offered a full line of fresh bread, cakes, and pies.

Front cover: *Horse-drawn carriages and wagons lined the street when the Commercial Block was the town's center of commerce. Much of the Commercial Block was destroyed in the 1901 fire.*

THE
MAKING OF AMERICA
SERIES

MATAWAN AND ABERDEEN
OF TOWN AND FIELD

HELEN HENDERSON
MATAWAN HISTORICAL SOCIETY

ARCADIA
PUBLISHING

Copyright © 2003 by Matawan Historical Society
ISBN 978-0-7385-2403-0

Published by Arcadia Publishing
Charleston SC, Chicago IL, Portsmouth NH, San Francisco CA

Printed in the United States

Library of Congress control number: 2002109312

For all general information contact Arcadia Publishing at:
Telephone 843-853-2070
Fax 843-853-0044
E-Mail sales@arcadiapublishing.com
For customer service and orders:
Toll-Free 1-888-313-2665

Visit us on the Internet at www.arcadiapublishing.com

DiSanto's corner, 1 Main Street, has changed drastically since this 1913 photo. Many commuters would not recognize the site of the train station parking lot. (Courtesy of the DiSanto family.)

CONTENTS

ACKNOWLEDGMENTS

Many people and institutions contributed to this work by loaning images and sharing their knowledge and reminiscences. This volume showcases the historical archives maintained by the Matawan Historical Society in the Burrowes Mansion Museum, as well as private and public collections. Some of the photographs are from the unpublished archives of the New Jersey Geological Survey, Department of Environmental Protection. Images with no acknowledgment in the caption are from the author's private collection, the archives of the Matawan Historical Society, or from a private collector who does not desire individual acknowledgment. All contributions to this work, whether great or small, were all gratefully appreciated.

A diligent effort was made to acknowledge those who made a contribution: Aberdeen Township Historical Commission; Anne V. Ambrosio; Aviation Hall of Fame and Museum of New Jersey; Robert and Cindy Bentley; Bob Chevalier; Richard Dalton; J.C. Erickson Jr.; Tom Gallo; The Freedom Forum; Edward Fitzgerald; Grace Graupe-Pillard; Joseph Greco; Regina Hawn; Howard and Elizabeth Henderson; Thomas H. Henderson; Edward D. Hyrne; Gail Hunton; Madison Township Historical Society, Matawan-Aberdeen Free Public Library; Garrett and Mary McKeen; Monmouth County Park System; Ralph Phillips; Susan Pike; New Jersey Geological Survey, Department of Environmental Protection; North Jersey Electric Railway Historical Society; Willett A. Rhodes; Carmen Rodriguez; Councilwoman Sharon Roselli; Gerard Scharfenberger; Scott Stanford; Anita Stratos; Glenn Vogel; and Dina and Louis Zampelle. Apologies to any who may have inadvertently been omitted.

INTRODUCTION

"Matawan is nevertheless a pleasant, solid looking village, and a desirable place of residence. Some of the houses show signs of great age, but on the other hand it possesses many large, modern-built cottages. . . . The sidewalks are paved with flagstone and brick."

~ Editor, *Long Branch News*, 1875

Penned in 1875, the above quote describes the area that is now Aberdeen Township and Matawan Borough. The history of Matawan and Aberdeen from their humble beginnings over 300 years ago to the turn of the twenty-first century is briefly told herein. While this work may detail the history of what became two municipal entities, ever since the first settlers arrived and laid out farms and a village, the histories of Aberdeen Township and Matawan Borough have been intricately entwined. Although for much of their existence the township and the borough shared the same name, each has its own unique character. This work attempts to show both the commonality and the uniqueness of each area, the rich and varied history of what was once referred to as "the Matawans," the people who forged it, and the diverse industry that has taken place there.

The Matawans have always been unique. According to the Federal Writers Project 1936 history of Matawan, Minnesota had the only other post office with that name in the United States. First cousins once or twice removed are Mattawan, Michigan and Matewan, West Virginia, better known as the site of the famous feud between the Hatfields and the McCoys. Located at the northern tip of Monmouth County, Matawan Borough is 2.26 square miles, surrounded on three sides by Aberdeen Township. Bounded on the east by the Raritan Bay, Aberdeen Township is 5.4 square miles. The township shares borders with Keyport Borough and Marlboro, Hazlet, and Holmdel Townships. Like the borough, the township also shares a border with Middlesex County. The 1936 history (both the township and borough were named Matawan back then), listed three communities in the township: Cliffwood Beach, Cliffwood, and Oak Shades. Since then, the building of several housing developments, including Strathmore, Contempra, River Gardens, and Marc Woods, have in essence contributed additional communities to the borough and township.

The VanBrakle farm, one of the longest-held properties in Monmouth County, was owned by the same family from 1709 to 2002. The farm, shown here c. 1890, is on VanBrackle Road in Aberdeen. (Courtesy of the Bentley family.)

By the time the colonies declared their independence from Great Britain, the area around Matawan, then called Middletown Point, had been settled by European émigrés for almost 100 years. It was a small village of less than 100 dwellings. As Matawan and Aberdeen entered the twenty-first century, the population of the borough hovered just below 9,000. The population of 17,454 reported for the township illustrates just how much the area has changed from its early history when the suburban home developments of today were farm fields and wooded areas.

This book is intended as a companion volume to the pictorial history *Around Matawan and Aberdeen*. Therefore, many of the photographs appropriate for this book were already published in the prior work. Other images of buildings, events, or organizations may have been excluded due to limited space or lack of a quality image. Extra care has been taken to include within these pages various aspects of the area's history that have been neglected or omitted by other works such as *Matawan 1686–1936*. This book was written under the auspices of the Matawan Historical Society, a non-profit organization created in 1969 to preserve the history of what was once called Middletown Point. The society operates the Burrowes Mansion Museum as one of its projects. The building itself, along with several other historic sites in town—the Mt. Pleasant Cemetery, Philip Freneau's gravesite, and the St. James AME Zion Church Historical Cemetery—are owned by the Borough of Matawan and managed by the Historic Sites Commission.

History is a work in progress. It is constantly changing with new facts uncovered, commonly-held stories proved to be folklore, and perceptions changed. When commenting on writing an early history of Matawan, Judge William Spader noted back in 1876, "Absence of archives and records made reliance on old timers a necessity." When you rely on human memory, variations appear, even in the anecdotes of recent memory. Discrepancies in dates or the spelling of names can be found among various sources, especially in the early history of the town. The mists of time had already hidden some information from the researchers of 100 years ago; so, those of today must take some information on faith, while using other data, such as that provided by archeology, to make current histories as accurate and informative as possible. Many years' worth of research is included in this volume, both by the author and by others who have delved in-depth into specific topics. Although every effort has been made to ensure the accuracy of this book, apologies are given in advance for any errors that may be herein. But as any author will tell, what is known today may be disproved tomorrow.

One of the major landmarks of the borough is the 1870s blue Victorian at 226 Main Street (shown here in 2002), built by textile merchant D.G. Ryer. Beautifully restored, it is Monmouth County's finest example of the French Second Empire style. (Courtesy of Anne V. Ambrosio.)

1. Geography and Prehistory

The history of Matawan-Aberdeen can be traced back about 10 million years to the last marine inundation of the coastal plain, to a time before the land area now known as New Jersey began to emerge from beneath a prehistoric sea. Matawan-Aberdeen is located in the physiographic region of New Jersey called the Inner Coastal Plain, one of six regions in the state. The plain stretches from the Raritan Bay in the northeast, diagonally across the state to the Delaware River near the top of the Delaware Bay. Sand, clay, and marls deposited during the Tertiary Period of the Cenozoic Era and the Cretaceous Period of the Mesozoic Era lie beneath the plain—a natural resource that would later form the basis for major industry. The landscape was later affected by climatic activity with additional deposits of sand and gravel formed during the Ice Ages. As the great ice sheet that covered much of North America retreated, the water that flowed from the glacier caused the sea level to rise.

Geologic investigations of New Jersey, including the coastal plain, published by Henry D. Rogers in 1840, George H. Cook in 1868, and more detailed investigations in 1891, laid the groundwork for the use of stratigraphic divisions. Geographic names were later substituted for the stratigraphic by naming formations, distinctive bodies of sedimentary rock that can be mapped on the basis of their composition, after the location where they were exposed. Previously known as "the clay marl series," the term "Matawan" was first suggested in 1894 as a name for the glauconite sands exposed along Matawan Creek. Some formations are further classified as being part of a group. At first regarded as a formation, the Matawan was later raised to the rank of a group with individual members, such as the Englishtown, being called formations. Overlying the Raritan Formation, the Matawan group consists of the Wenonah, Marshalltown, Englishtown, Woodbury, and Merchantville Formations. Hazlet sands and Crosswick clays comprise the group.

First used by N.H. Darton in 1893 for exposures along the Magothy River, which runs into the Chesapeake Bay, the name Magothy Formation supplanted the local name of "Cliffwood Clays" used for the fossil-bearing material exposed along the Raritan Bay at Cliffwood. In the vicinity of the Raritan Bay, the Raritan Formation can be easily distinguished from the overlying Magothy. Because

One of the area's major geologic formations, the Magothy, was exposed in a clay pit of a Cliffwood brick works (photo c. 1931). (Courtesy of the New Jersey Geological Survey.)

the separation is much more difficult to make further to the southwest, many geological maps combine the two formations. The Magothy Formation extends across New Jersey from the Raritan Bay to the Delaware Memorial Bridge.

Eons before the first European explorers sailed up the Raritan Bay toward what was to become Matawan, the area was inhabited by other creatures now lost in the passage of time. Remnants of these early inhabitants can occasionally be found in the bluffs of Cliffwood Beach. William B. Gallagher wrote in *When Dinosaurs Roamed New Jersey,* "For genuine Mesozoic amber containing prehistoric insects, New Jersey is one of the best spots in the world." The fossilized tree resin preserved whatever was trapped in the sap, such as spiders, ants, bees, or other insects. Although the discoveries in the amber dug from the Sayre and Fisher pit in Sayreville, New Jersey are probably the most well known, Cliffwood Beach was also a source of fossil-bearing amber. Found in amber along the shore at Cliffwood Beach, near an outcrop of the Magothy Formation, are some of the oldest known ants.

In 1965, Mr. and Mrs. Edmund Frey sent a piece of amber they discovered at Cliffwood Beach to Donald Baird of Princeton University, who recognized its scientific importance. The piece was investigated by authorities on insect paleontology at Harvard and Cornell Universities. Captured in the fossilized resin of the sequoia trees that grew in the Cliffwood Beach locality 90 million years ago were two worker ants, preserved as though the insects had only been entombed the day before. The insects were named *Sphecomyrma freyi*: the generic name *Sphecomyrma* meaning "wasp ant" and *freyi* honoring the couple that found them.

Prior to the discovery of *sphecomyrma*, the known fossil record had stopped in the Eocene sediments some 40 to 60 million years ago. Entomologist Edward O. Wilson of Harvard was quoted in 1998 in the *Washington Post* as saying, "the new find places the insects so far back in time that we now know the ants were stinging dinosaurs." Although originally classified as a wasp ant, further research by a team of entomologists from the American Museum of Natural History in New York City and the discovery of a metapleural gland in the amber-encased ants have since determined that *sphecomyrma* should be considered an ant.

Sphecomyrma was not the only special ant found at Cliffwood Beach. David Grimaldi, head of the museum's department of entomology and co-author of the paper on the initial discovery of *sphecomyrma*, is quoted in a *Washington Post* article that the discovery in amber of a worker ant from a much more modern ant subfamily promises to be even more significant. The importance of the second find is that if such an advanced ant existed approximately 92 million years ago, it could mean that the first primitive ants actually evolved many millions of years before. Members of the genus Ponerinae can still be found in the tropics today.

Ants in amber are not the only fossil record that can be found in the Matawan-Aberdeen area. Fossils have been found in the bluff along the bay, in loose material on the beach, in the clay pits for the various brickyards, and along the banks of the Matawan and Cheesequake Creeks. Extensive marine fauna has been observed in the sand and clay beds in the formation near Cliffwood. Elsewhere in the

The rich deposits of clay and green marl not only supported development of the ceramic tile and brick industries, but provided a fossil record of prehistoric fauna and flora. This image shows a stiff mud brick–making machine at Farry's Brick Yard, c. 1902. (Courtesy of the New Jersey Geological Survey.)

township, plant and other non-marine fossils have been found. Some fossils, such as the *Trigonarca cliffwoodensis* Weller, have a local name as part of their designation because of their discovery in the Matawan-Aberdeen area. In the late 1880s, Dr. Samuel Lockwood discovered the remains of a mosasaur in the clay banks of Cliffwood. According to avocational archeologist Ralph Phillips, fossilized shark teeth and the vertebrae from a mosasaur have been found in the gravel quarry just off Route 34. He said the quarry was a major fossil hunting site in the mid-1950s to late 1960s. In *The Cretaceous Fossils of New Jersey*, Horace G. Richards wrote of the finding of numerous tubes of *Halyminites major* and a few obsessive mollusks in a road cut 1.5 miles south of Matawan on the east side of Route 34. In *Fossils of New Jersey*, James S. Yolton wrote that "sharks teeth occur in great numbers in sandy deposits on the east side of Rt. 34 one mile south of Matawan."

Long before the European settlers came to the Raritan Bay, the area was already the site of human inhabitation. Because the time of the Lenape and their ancestors was unlike modern times, and was without detailed political boundaries and permanent populations, much of the history of the Native Americans in the Matawan-Aberdeen area cannot be separated from their history elsewhere in the state. Additionally, considering the volumes that have been written on the Delaware, the Lenape, and other groups in the Mid-Atlantic area that includes New Jersey, the history is necessarily abbreviated herein.

While many residents of the area have heard of the Lenape, much information on them has been lost, is inaccurate, or does not apply to the inhabitants of the Matawan-Aberdeen area. Early accounts of the Lenape and their culture were written by casual observers who had not lived among the Native Americans for any length of time. Because the early documents deal, for the most part, with the regions in and around New York Bay, the Hudson River, and the Delaware River, little or no information was recorded about the Atlantic coastal area from Staten Island to Cape May. As a result, a lot of what is known today has been obtained through archeological research.

In one of his books, Herbert C. Kraft, noted authority on the Native American inhabitants of New Jersey, defined archeology, if properly done, as "the re-creation of extinct cultures, the rediscovery of how a particular people lived in the past." In 1986, Kraft wrote the following:

> Although archeology has made extraordinary progress in the past fifty years and continues to improve, there is still much about the Lenape Indians and their pre-historic ancestors that archeology may never be able to uncover.

In the almost 20 years since that statement was written, additional archaeological discoveries near Matawan have expanded knowledge of the Lenape and their ancestors. The archaeological research is continuing, however; as Kraft states, there is still much that is unknown. In the centuries since European exploration of what became New Jersey, thousands upon thousands of Native American artifacts, such as arrowheads, spear points, axes, net sinkers, and potshards, have been found by farmers plowing their fields, in casual discovery, and by collectors of Native American relics. Many such items were found in Aberdeen Township when farm fields dominated the landscape.

Like other Native American tribes, the Lenape were victims of circumstance. Their pastoral existence changed due to contact with a people of different religious convictions and culture. Decimated by pestilence and war, uprooted and driven from their homeland, the Lenape and their Munsee-speaking kinsmen ultimately dispersed and reestablished themselves in other parts of the North American continent. They left behind an indelible mark on what was once Lenapehoking, or Land of the Lenape. Tribal names and words appear on modern maps as towns, streets names, and geographical features, as well as the names of creeks and rivers. In fact, the name of Matawan is derived from a Native American word.

Several meanings have been given for "Matawan." Depending on the source, it has been taken to mean "where two rivers come together," referring to the Matawan and Gravelly Creeks, and "elevated tract of land on either side." The meaning most frequently used is "meeting place of brothers," a reference to the crossing of the Chingarora and Minisink trails in the area. There were also branch paths from Matawan to Keyport and to Cliffwood Beach. A trail went from Matawan to Freehold via Wickatunk. At Freehold, it joined the Burlington Path, which led over towards the Delaware River. The 1945 reprint of the 1938 New Jersey Writers Project of the Work Projects Administration compilation of current and extinct names in New Jersey lists "mechawanienk" as a Native American name for Matawan. Mechawanienk was given to mean "ancient path." The word Matawan can be traced to the word Matovancons, a name given to one of the Indian tribes by early Dutch explorers and traders. An early reference to the name is found on the A. Vanderdonck 1656 map of Nieuw Netherland. The Federal Writers Project 1936 history of Matawan states that Dutch settlers referred to the Matawan area as Muttovang, while the 1683 purchase of land from the Native Americans by the surveyor general Thomas Rudyard referred to the area as Mittevang. Native American names have been recorded for more than just the town. Nashinakime was written as the Native American name for the Matawan Creek.

There have been human inhabitants in the area for approximately 10,000 years. Various groups are identified by either the archeological era in which they inhabited the land or by the names they called themselves. Since archaeologists do not know what the prehistoric Native Americans called themselves, they have devised names including Paleo-Indians and early or late Woodland Indians. The term "Delaware" is reserved for the Unami-speaking people of the late seventeenth, eighteenth, and nineteenth centuries and their descendents.

According to Kraft, the Paleo-Indians were physically modern humans and generally lived to between 30 and 35 years of age. Among these early hunting and gathering people, there were no permanent leaders or chiefs. Decisions were probably made in consultation with headmen and elders, and by consensus.

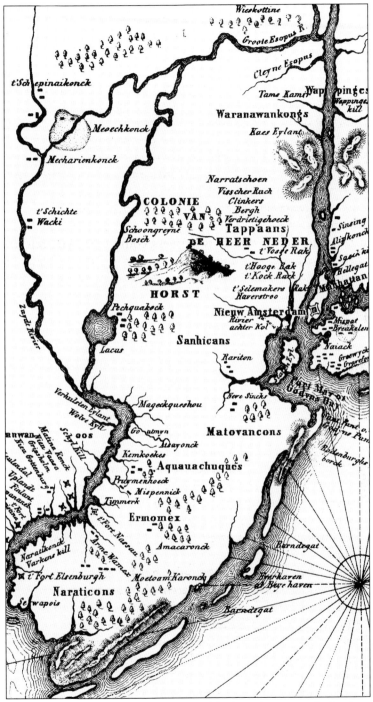

The name "Matawan" can be traced back to the A. Vanderdonck c. 1656 map, which recorded the local residents as Matovancons.

Among the evidence of early residents' visits to the shore are shell middens (shell heaps) found at individual campsites in the Matawan-Aberdeen area. (Courtesy of the New Jersey State Museum.)

Although hunter-gatherers, the Paleo-Indians were already in possession of a fairly sophisticated tool technology. They had the ability to make fire and sew tailored skin clothing and skin boots to preserve body heat and prevent frostbite in the cold northern climate. Over the course of a few thousand years, they had explored many of the available habitable regions of the Western Hemisphere. Important Paleo-Indian sites have been discovered in New Jersey, Pennsylvania, New York, and elsewhere in the northeastern United States. With one of the sites in nearby Freehold, New Jersey, Paleo-Indians can be considered the first human inhabitants of the Matawan-Aberdeen area. There is no way to know precisely when the first humans arrived in the Atlantic coastal area; however, since 1950 archaeologists have been able to date several prehistoric sites by means of carbon-14 or radiocarbon dating from about 10,000 to 12,000 years ago.

The landscape, when the Paleo-Indians first began to explore the Mid-Atlantic coastal area, was different from today. The coasts of New Jersey, New York, Pennsylvania, and Delaware extended more than 50 miles east of the present shoreline. A broad, exposed continental shelf was cut by deep river channels. As the global warming trend increased, the Wisconsin glacier slowly retreated north, releasing enormous volumes of water. Gradually, the ocean deepened, overflowing the lowlands. By 12,000 B.C., the glacier had retreated north of the headwaters of the Delaware River.

By 9000 B.C., small bands of Paleo-Indian hunters and gatherers had already been living in the Mid-Atlantic region for several thousand years. It has become fairly commonly accepted that human beings were living here at the same time as mammoth, mastodon, caribou, musk oxen, moose elk, giant beaver, and the dire wolf. Although now either extinct or no longer found in this area, the remains of these animals have been excavated from bogs and dredged from the continental shelf off New Jersey and adjacent states. As clovis-like fluted spearpoints have been found in New Jersey similar to those found embedded in the bones of mammoths and bison out west, it is reasonable to assume human hunters killed and ate such animals in the east as was done out west. The Mashantucket Pequot Museum and Research Center in Mashantucket, Connecticut has an interactive exhibit illustrating such a hunt using migrating caribou as the prey.

A precursor of the Lenape were the Woodland and Archaic cultures in the eastern United States. The Archaic Period is delineated as between 8000 B.C. and 1000 B.C. During this time period, the human inhabitants were still primarily hunter-gatherers, although they also fished and ate crustaceans and assorted shellfish that lived along the coast, in bays, and in estuaries. The bands were isolated from each other and moved frequently, except when food was plentiful. Two facts lend credence to the theory that these hunter-gatherer bands were made up of small numbers of people: the sparcity of evidence from the time period, and the fact that the levels of game and edible plants were insufficient to support large populations. Before most of the melting of the remnant of the Wisconsin glacier finished around approximately 6000 B.C., the sea level rose as much as 1 foot per century. As rising water levels changed the coastline and flooded flat areas, plant, animal, and human populations were forced inland and had to adapt. Flooding can also account for the lack of archeological evidence.

Among the innovations of the Archaic Period was an improvement in tool technology with the discovery that certain kinds of sedimentary and metamorphic stones, if properly shaped, could be converted into very useful heavy-duty woodworking tools. Prior to the middle of the Archaic Period, these stones were primarily used as anvil stones, net sinkers, or throwing stones. During the later part of the period, as the population increased steadily, encampments became correspondingly larger and more numerous. Hunting, fishing, and gathering were still the principal day-to-day activities, although a greater emphasis was placed on small game, shellfish, nuts, and wild cereal grains. Freshwater mussels from inland streams such as the Raritan River were almost certainly eaten. Clams and oysters required little or no specialized equipment for harvesting, could be obtained at any time the rivers were not frozen, were eaten raw or smoked, and were stored for use during the winter months. Large shell middens have been found on both sides of the Hudson River, across the Raritan Bay at Tottenville in Staten Island, and in the Cheesequake area. Other middens, such as the one that existed many years ago near Keyport, no longer exist, having been washed away or carried away by farmers to neutralize the acidity in the soil of their fields. Small shell middens have been found by Ralph Phillips at individual campsites in the Matawan-Aberdeen area.

It was also during the later portion of the Archaic Period that the mortar and pestle appeared as a food-processing tool, although no cooking pots of stone or pottery were in use. According to Kraft, "Fishing must have been important to the people of the Late Archaic times, because so many of their camp sites were located near large rivers, estuaries, and coasts." With its various creeks and access to the Raritan Bay, the Matawan-Aberdeen area could have provided suitable campsites to these early inhabitants.

The Lenape were Woodland Indians. Although there are references to the Lenni Lenape, for this work the more modern usage of Lenape is used throughout. The term woodland does not necessarily mean that they lived in wooded land, but pertains to the prehistoric Woodland Era that Kraft classifies as between 1000 B.C. and 1600 A.D. Lenape is a word from the Unami dialect of the language of the Delaware Indians. Unami means "person from down under." Among the various meanings for Lenape are "a male of our kind," "our men," "men of the same nation," or "common," "ordinary," or "real people." According to Kraft, it does not mean "original people" in the sense that many writers have defined it in the past.

The geography and climate of the Woodland Period was similar to that of today. By the late Woodland Era, Algonquin Indians (of which the Lenape were a part) along the entire Atlantic Coast were using bows and arrows for hunting. Among the major developments of the Woodland Era was the introduction of pottery. Early vessels were soapstone (steatite) or talc. Kettles made from these soft stones were easily carved with chisels and scrapers. Pottery vessels also came into use during the later part of the period. Throughout the late Woodland Era, pottery vessels were made in a variety of shapes and sizes to serve as cooking and storage pots, and receptacles for water. Coil construction was an early method of pottery. Pottery vessels made by the proto-Unami Indians of central and southern New Jersey, southeastern Pennsylvania, and northern Delaware were not collared. Clay was the essential ingredient and could be obtained from the riverbanks. Usually the clay was pulverized, sifted, and stored until needed. A temper of crushed stone, sand, or shell was used to help stabilize the clay and keep it from cracking during the firing process.

The lives, fortunes, and ancient ways of the Lenape were changed forever by contact with European explorers in the sixteenth century, and with the traders and settlers who followed. C.A. Weslager published the following account of the coming of the white man to the Delaware as recounted to a young Lenape boy by a wise man:

> Some of the men of our village were fishing at a place where the sea widens. They saw something big floating on the water, and it kept coming toward them. At first it looked like a large fish or a bird with white wings. Then they saw it was a big house that moved on the water.

The Lenape who frequented the Matawan-Aberdeen area might have seen such a site from the bluffs of Cliffwood. The story continues that the braves notified the chief, who told them it must be the house where Manito the Great Spirit lived and the tribe welcomed the white explorers with meat, fish, and corn.

The gorget in the center of the arrangement was found in a peach orchard in Freneau near the Freneau gravesite monument and is flanked by the drill stones that made the holes and projectile points. (Courtesy of Ralph Phillips.)

The earliest recorded European journey to Lenapehoking was in 1524 when Giovanni da Verrazano skirted the northeastern coast and briefly entered New York Bay. The real exploration and settlement of the land of the Lenape began in 1609 with the third voyage of Henry Hudson. Kraft wrote that incidents of slave raids, kidnapping, and other unfriendly acts were doubtless reported from one tribe to another up and down the east coast so that, "There was most likely considerable Lenape mistrust of the Europeans by the time Henry Hudson and the crew of the *Half Moon* entered New York Bay and the Hudson River on September 3, 1609."

Like other Algonquin tribes, the Lenape traded with the Europeans. Animal skins, such as beaver, were traded for a variety of objects. Metal objects were especially desirable for their sharp edges, durability, and usability. Metal axes felled trees more quickly, while simplifying construction of deadfalls and spring traps. Brass pots were also treasured as they did not break like the pottery jars and pots, and could be hung over a fire by their handle. Eventually, the animal population was decimated, reducing the levels of trade. Kraft writes that by 1644, trade had declined to a point where the Lenape were seriously restricted in bartering for trade goods, some of which had become necessary for daily activities. In 1644, Johan Printz, governor of New Sweden, observed, "we have no beaver trade with them, but only the maize trade."

One of the most commonly known stories of Native American life, and possibly one of the most misunderstood, is that of wampum. Among the prehistoric Lenape, beads were an item of adornment and were made from shells, fruit pits, bones, or soft stone. However, such beads were not plentiful and very few have survived in the archeological record. The confusion of shell beads with the later wampum is a common misconception. Wampum was made from a specific type of shell bead. As they were forbidden by their respective governments to coin money in the New World, wampum was used by the Dutch and English traders as a medium of exchange acceptable both to the Native Americans and the colonists, and an elaborate exchange system was developed.

Local lore has it that the Lenape traveled to the Matawan-Aberdeen region to make wampum from the Chingarora oysters. Charles A. Philhower wrote, "Indian bands from the interior and as far away as Minisink Island traveled to South Jersey for seafood and shells for wampum beads. Indians would return north with backloads of dried and smoked oysters and clams together with quantities of shell beads made over the summer." Current information tends to discount the lore. According to Kraft, "It is unlikely Indians would have traveled 100 miles or more to get shellfish when there were fresh water mussels in the rivers." Another point he makes is that wampum beads did not become important until the colonial period when they could be made with iron drills introduced by the Europeans. The majority of the Lenape who had inhabited the Matawan-Aberdeen area had already been displaced by then. Kraft also points out that wampum was made by the Narragansett and other coastal New England tribes and that the Lenape made practically no wampum. Writings by Printz that he had to go to Manhattan to buy wampum casts doubt on the wampum lore.

However, it should be kept in mind that much of Kraft's research and archaeological work was focused on the tribes along the Delaware River and Printz was head of New Sweden, also on the western side of the state. The Native Americans who lived in the Matawan-Aberdeen area were much closer to Nieuw Amsterdam (now New York) for trade. With access to the Raritan Bay through

Oysters were used as food by Native Americans and later settlers, who after processing them in kilns such as this one, used the shells to neutralize the acidity in the soil of their fields. (Courtesy of the Monmouth County Park System.)

Wigwams for shelter were made using saplings and wooden shingles. (Courtesy of the New Jersey State Museum.)

Keyport and Cliffwood, the local tribes could have made shell beads from the shellfish once plentiful in the bay. According to Phillips, "it was said that many years ago the remains of Indian wampum makers' workshops could still be found on the shores of the Raritan Bay."

A direct consequence of European trade and contact was the spread of virulent diseases against which the Native Americans had no natural immunity. Measles, smallpox, scarlet fever, typhus, and influenza were among the diseases that ravaged the native inhabitants of the coastal regions and destroyed communities.

The Native Americans of Lenapehoking began adjusting and relocating with the first European settlement in the region. Small groups were already moving westward as early as 1690, when a portion of the Minsis who had settled among the Ottawas had joined the French Alliance. As more settlers arrived with every ship, their impact on the land and the Native Americans intensified. Woodlands were cut for timber or cleared for farms and pastures. The Lenape's familiar environment with natural food resources was being replaced by houses, barns, taverns, mills, and wharfs. After the Walking Purchase Treaty of 1737, most of the Minisink and the other Munsee-speaking people moved to the west as well. Scholars estimate the entire Lenape population may have only been 8,000 to 12,000 at the time of European contact. By the time of the French and Indian War (1754–1763), the total number of Lenape in the state was less than 1,000.

Among the bands that remained in New Jersey and preserved a sense of identity into the twentieth century are the Sand Hill Delaware, a Monmouth County group composed of Lenape descendents, immigrant Cherokees, African Americans, and whites. By 1877, the group's carpentry and craftsman skills were in such demand in the developing shore communities that they developed their own settlement in Whitesville (now Neptune). The community came to be known as Sand Hill.

2. PRESBYTERIANS PIONEER AT MATAWAN

European settlement of the Matawan-Aberdeen area began in the late 1680s. The settlers picked the area for several reasons: the soil was rich for growing vegetables, fruit orchards, and grain crops; the Native American paths would form the beginnings of a road system; and the creeks were to be a major transportation resource. The earliest English land grant in Aberdeen was made in 1677, when Sir George Carteret granted 36 acres on Mohingson Creek in present-day Oak Shades to Jonathan Holmes. In 1684, Surveyor General Thomas Rudyard received a grant of 1,038 acres on Raritan Bay and Matawan Creek, the present location of Cliffwood and Cliffwood Beach. Owing to Rudyard's high office, the grant was quite controversial and, in 1685, the board of proprietors issued an order regarding the laying out of land. Part of the order addressed questionable activity such as Rudyard's. He then sold his land to his son-in-law Samuel Winder.

On September 30, 1686, the date that would be used 300 years later by Matawan Borough and Township as the official date of its founding, the Proprietors of East New Jersey granted 400 acres to Stephen Warne and his son Thomas. Warne's Neck, as the tract was subsequently called, included the land between Matawan and Gravel (Gravelly Brook) Creeks and later became the central portion of Matawan Borough and part of the southwestern tip of Aberdeen Township. Warne had previously acquired 1,000 acres of land on the north side of Matawan Creek (present-day Old Bridge Township). He was also supposed to have erected a wigwam on Warne's Neck in 1685, earning him the title of the area's first white settler.

Another prominent figure in Monmouth County history was Captain John Bowne, one of the original recipients of land grants issued by the royal governor Colonel Richard Nicolls in the Monmouth Patent. In 1683, the combined real estate holdings of John Bowne, his brother Andrew, and John's sons John Jr. and Obadiah totaled almost 10,000 acres throughout the area. Bowne land nearly surrounded what would become Middletown Point. When he died in 1684, his widow Lydia Holmes Bowne received the homestead with all buildings and improvements. She later received a grant from the Proprietors of East New

Jersey of 500 acres of land on Matawan Creek between Gravelly Brook and Mohingson Creek.

The arrival of Scotch Presbyterians was the first major development of the Matawan-Aberdeen area. During a period of Scotland's history known as the "killing times," the Black Watch of King Charles II swept over Scotland seeking the Covenanters, who were mainly Scotch Presbyterians who hated prelacy. Ellis L. Derry wrote about the Covenanters in *In Old and Historic Churches of New Jersey*, "For 28 years from 1660 to 1688 they were hunted down, thrown into prison, sold as slaves, banished from the country, their property taken from them." It is estimated that 18,000 Covenanters were either killed or banished.

A group of Covenanters arrived in the New World in 1685 on the *Henry and Francis*, a 350-ton, 20-gun ship. Unlike the pilgrims who voluntarily sailed from Plymouth, England, the Covenanters had been banished from the Scotch Highlands. Most came to the colonies as bonded or indentured servants to George Scott, Laird of Pitlochie. Scott himself had been confined in the tollbooth of Leith because he wouldn't take the Oath of Allegiance to the King. In addition to those banished, Dr. William M. Glasgow documented a list of people who voluntarily left Scotland on the *Henry and Francis* in his history of the Reformed Presbyterian Church in America. Among the passengers who sailed not because of banishment, but for some other reason, were Lady Athunie, Reverend William Aisdale, William Ged, Dr. John Johnstone (an Edinburgh druggist), George Scot, Margaret Scot, Eupham Scot, John Vernor, Mrs. Vernor, William Rigg, and Reverend and Mrs. Archibald Riddell.

While not the old growth forest that would have greeted the early settlers, some wooded areas still remain, especially in gullies, such as that seen in this early 1900s photocard. Many of the later tree stands have been leveled for homes.

This image shows the intersection of Main and Church Streets in 1912. The settlement of Mt. Pleasant eventually developed into a small town where Main Street was the heart of commerce and transportation.

After serving out their term of service, the original settlers were to receive a land grant according to their indenture. The base grant was 25 acres, with tradesmen receiving 30 acres at a cost of 2d (pennies) an acre. The typical term of an indenture service was four years, beginning with the servant's arrival in America. The bonded servants were to perform the services the person holding the indenture thought fit. In consideration for the term of service, the master agreed to pay for the servant's passage to the colonies and other considerations such as those described in a period indenture between David ffergusen, merchant in Edinburgh, and Euphan Lewis, indweller in Edinburgh. David ffergusen agreed to the following:

> find for and allow her meat, drink, apparrell, lodging and all other
> necessarys from the date hereof and during the space of this indenture
> and to give her the ordinary allowance of the country after the expiration
> hereof according to the custom of the Country in the like kind.

Scott started out with 125 prisoners, of whom 31 died on the voyage. In all, 60 passengers and crew died during the 15-week Atlantic crossing, including the laird and his wife. The laird's death did not automatically mean the survivors were free from their bonded servitude. The laird's daughter Euphemia survived the trip and married fellow passenger Dr. John Johnstone. Johnstone tried to persuade the surviving bonded passengers to give him the four years of service owed the laird, but they refused. A court subsequently ruled that their only obligation was to pay passage claims by Captain Richard Hutton of the *Henry and Francis*. Since Perth Amboy was the colonial capitol and the Scotch of New Aberdeen were closely allied by kindred and nationality to the settlers of Perth Amboy, it is reasonable that the survivors of the *Henry and Francis* spent some time there acclimating to the New World before making their way to what is now known as Matawan and Freneau. By several accounts, a number of the immigrants served out some of their indenture before leaving the Perth Amboy area.

According to historian James Steen in his 1899 history of New Aberdeen, between 1687 and 1689, 24 of the Scotch Presbyterians purchased land and built a settlement. Some records refer to the settlement as New Aberdeen. Other records, including a 1701 survey, refer to the area as Mt. Pleasant. Steen noted that the deed for the land is dated, "as was to have been expected, some years after the actual settlement" as was the case in other towns in Monmouth and elsewhere. The land upon which the town of New Aberdeen was built is described by the surveyor John Reid in records at the secretary of state's office in Trenton:

> All that hundred ackers of land adjoyneing upon the south side of land late of Andrew Burnet formerly Thomas Warn's and bounded easterly by land lots of Thomas Hart, granted to these persons by patent from the proprietors of East New Jersey bearing date the seventh day of June, Anno Dom, 1701, beginning at a stake on the line of Warne's land, being a corner of said Hart's and twelve chains from Gravell Brook and running along the Rear of said Hart's land south twenty degrees East Leaven chaine; then South three degrees West six chaine, then South Twenty degrees East two chain and one Rod to a stake and corner of Lewis Nisbett's land then South Seaventy-three degrees West Seaventy-two chaine, then North ten degrees West to the line of said Warne's land and then alonge his line North Seaventy three degrees East to where it began.

The settlement at Mt. Pleasant was expanded in 1700 when several of the original settlers, along with some later newcomers to the community, purchased 2 additional acres on Matawan Creek. Docks and storage sheds were built on the site. The deed for the wharf recorded the description of the tract:

> All that small tract of land on the east side of Matawan Creek beginning at a small red oak tree, near the creek at the upper-end of the second point of meadow (and about twenty chains on a straight line from the point of the neck) and running south-east four degrees more southerly eight chains. Thence south-west and half a point more southerly two chains and two rods. Thence north-west and four degrees more northerly to the said creek and thence down the creek to where it began.

Using a June 7, 1701 survey and December 1684 lists of imported servants of record in Trenton as the basis, James Steen created a list of the original landholders. Allowing for some discrepancies in the interpretation of the spelling of the names, the original landholders were: Alexander Colwell (Caldwell), Alexander Napier, Charles Gordon, James Reid, James Edward, James Melven (Melvin), John Brown, John Baird, John Campbell, John Hamton (Heonton), John Nelson, John Nesmith, John Reid, Patrick Canaan (Kinnan), Patrick Emlay (Imlay), Peter Watson, Dr. John Johnstone, Robert Ray (Rhea?), Walter Ker, William Clark, William Laing (Layng), William Naughty, William Redford, and William Ronald (Ronnol).

One of the most significant of the early landholders was John Reid, born February 13, 1655 at Midrew Castle, Kirkliston Parish, Scotland. Although the family had been gardeners for several generations, Reid was apprenticed out at age 12 to an Edinburgh wine dealer. He sailed for the New World from Aberdeen, Scotland in August 1683 and became a deputy surveyor upon arrival in the colonies. It was Reid working under George Keith who drew up the dividing line between East and West New Jersey. Reid learned the surveyor trade well, and in 1703 was appointed surveyor-general of the province. Alexander Napier came to the colonies to work off a four-year indenture. Originally a Presbyterian, he changed his religious affiliations several times during his lifetime, worshiping as both a Quaker and an Episcopalian. Per Woodrow's Scottish church records, John Campbell was banished from Scotland, forcing his emmigration to the New World. Not all of the original landowners of New Aberdeen were Presbyterians. Hamton was a Quaker before coming to the colonies. Several overseers sailed with the indentured servants to assist in managing the land and indentured servants. Serving a four-year indenture, John Hamton came over in 1683 on the ship *Exchange* and was one of David Barclay's overseers. Peter Watson, one of whose descendents was to achieve national fame during the American Revolution, is also supposed to have been an overseer.

Although his was the first name on the grant from the proprietors, according to Steen, Dr. John Johnstone was generally considered a resident of Perth Amboy. At least in his later years he resided there and died there in September 1732. However, Johnstone did have several ties to Monmouth County. His obituary in the *Philadelphia Weekly Mercury* reported that he may have lived part of his life in Monmouth County. His name was the first in the deed for Old Tennent and his marriage is recorded there. Steen states that Johnstone was residing in Monmouth County about 1710 when he was second judge of the Monmouth courts.

A large number of Scots, who were by no means exiles for conscience sake, came to Monmouth County between 1686 and 1700. Some found it advisable and convenient for political causes; some of broken fortunes sought to restore them; and the offer of real estate for settlers was by no means an insignificant motive. In 1688, the English middle classes triumphed in the revolution of that year and forced passage of a toleration act granting freedom of public worship to dissenters. That meant that political and religious motives, once quite strong, were now

In addition to Scotch Presbyterians, Dutch settlers also contributed to settling Matawan and Aberdeen. Several generations of VanBrakle women were captured on film. (Courtesy of the Bentley family.)

minimized. Other Scotsmen came at intervals, some of whom were Quakers and some of whom were Presbyterians.

The Scotch were not the only settlers in New Aberdeen. Steen also wrote about Scotch-Irish immigrants in his 1899 history of New Aberdeen. Although it was somewhat later, between 1718 and 1724, that Protestant-Irish first came in any large numbers. By the 1690s, Scotch immigration was in decline. In their place, Dutch settlers came to Monmouth County from New York, along with some Protestant French Huguenots. The population grew so much that an act passed in October 1693 created the first subdivision of Monmouth County, making Middletown, Shrewsbury, and Freehold Townships. What was to become Matawan and Aberdeen was part of Middletown Township and would remain so until 1848 when Raritan Township was formed.

Many of these new people came from Kings County, New York and were second- and third-generation descendents of the settlers of New Netherlands. By 1699, a church was established in what is now Marlboro Township. The Old Brick Reformed Church served as the center of a widespread community that included Matawan and Aberdeen. Families with names like Covenhoven (now Conover),

Schanck, Van Cleef, Vanderbilt, Vanderhoef, Van Brunt, and others were among the new residents. Large landowners included the Van Pelt and VanBrakle families in the southeastern part of Aberdeen Township. Between the two, William Hyer had a farm, while Peter Hyer owned a 38-acre farm near Mt. Pleasant. North of the VanBrakle farm, the LeQuiers had a 100-acre farm. The descendents of these Dutch settlers are still in Monmouth County, including Aberdeen and Matawan. Harry Perrine LeQuier served on the Matawan Borough Council in the 1970s and 1980s. Also, Matawan Mayor Robert D. Clifton is a direct linear descendent of Walter P. Hyer.

By 1707, tension in the colonies was severe due to the continued controversy between proprietors and early settlers over property rights, and the increasing numbers of Scots settling in the area and being elected to public office, thus becoming, in the eyes of the original English settlers, usurpers of power. According to the 1737 census, Monmouth County was the most populated county in East Jersey and the third most populated county in the state, which at the time was still divided into East and West New Jersey. The census recorded 1,508 white males above the age of 16, 1,339 white females above the age of 16, and 2,584 children. The census also reported 655 slaves, including children.

Life at Mt. Pleasant was primarily a rural lifestyle. Colonists had to reap and mow, and to thrash and glean. A sickle did the reaping as grain cradles were not

Built by Captain Joseph Chapman and for many years the home of Mayor Eggleston, this late eighteenth-century home at 222 Main Street, shown here in 1913, is one of the surviving Colonial-era homes. Of Federal architecture with colonial revival alternations, it has included parts from the Spafford Schanck house and paneling from the Matawan Library. (Courtesy of Regina Hawn.)

invented until 100 years later. Horses or oxen hooves trod out the corn and the winds winnowed it. Although Ernest W. Mandeville's comments in *The Story of Middletown: The Oldest Settlement in New Jersey* were written about the village of Middletown, as the settlement of Mt. Pleasant was part of Middletown at the time, they are illustrative of what life at Mt. Pleasant might have been like. Mandeville wrote about hogs running wild and fleas being in every house. Mosquitoes were complained about and called a "flying flea." Food was a mixture of beef, mutton, and game, and locally-grown crops such as wheat, rye, and corn or buckwheat flour, cabbage, pumpkins, and beans. Pork cured with salt from the Atlantic Ocean could be purchased for six shillings a bushel. Later, potatoes not only became a food crop, but a major cash crop of the area.

Mills, both grist and saw, were an important part of the early life of this sector of Monmouth County. Every farm in the locality at that time produced some grain crop, such as wheat, rye, oats, corn, and buckwheat. The grains were ground up into flour for the family's use. While some mills served only the immediate family, other mills ground flour or cut wood as a more commercial venture. There were a number of mills on or near Matawan Creek, some of which used the tidal action of the creek for power. The earliest of the mills was probably the Mount Pleasant Mill, opened around 1736 in the rear of what was formerly the Mount Pleasant Hotel. Located on Gravelly Brook, at one time the mill was used to produce linseed oil from locally-grown flax seed.

Mrs. Phoebe Hunn owned a sawmill in the 1700s. A 1799 deed from Thomas Hance to James Sergant refers to a gristmill on what became known as Wilson Avenue. In the nineteenth century, Jacob E. Wilson operated a mill on the site. Until the Township Committee changed the name to Wilson Avenue in 1925, the road was named Henninger's Mill Road. Johannes Hyer's sawmill stood a short distance downstream on the present Basilian Fathers' property.

Like all the rest of the early New Jersey settlers, until the proprietors surrendered the government to the Crown in 1702, the Scotch settlers of Monmouth County were ruled by British law under the control and government of the Proprietors of East New Jersey. Mandeville states there was a death penalty for over 200 crimes. Added to that penalty were different ingenious modes of inflicting death, such as whipping to death at the cart tail, breaking on the wheel, beheading and quartering, disemboweling, and burning at the stake. He continued, "Yet we find no case in the sentences of the Middletown courts but that of a negro, whose body was to be burned after death by hanging, and to show the simplicity of the times, the court met as early as six o'clock A.M." The penalty for political or religious offenses was slit noses, ear crops, or branding.

Although farming was the settlers' main occupation, most men also held public office at some time during their lives. Laws were established very early in the new communities springing up in Monmouth County and it was incumbent on the relatively few male citizens to take their turns at civic service, including juryman, constable, and court officer. However, not all duties were cheerfully accepted. In September 28, 1697, John Reid refused appointment as king's attorney for the

The Hunn-Hawkins house, at 19 Mill Road, is one of the few remaining pre-Revolutionary War structures left in the Matawan-Aberdeen area. Having served as a tavern during the Revolutionary War period, it is one of a select group of early Dutch houses in Monmouth County.

county. Steen noted that Reid "was duly fined forty shillings and commited by ye court 'to close gaole until he shall pay ye fine of fourty shillings.' "

In New Jersey, as elsewhere in the North, taverns or inns, referred to as houses in common usage, appeared almost as soon as settlements were made. In fact, the 1668 General Assembly ordered every town to provide an "ordinary," as the tavern or inn was called, "for the relief and entertainment of strangers." These inns were for more than food, drink, and lodging for travelers. They also served as the general meeting place of the community even for religious services, a site for the transaction of business, and a clearing-house for gossip and news.

Just south of the 100 acres upon which the original settlers of Mt. Pleasant were to build their town, Lewis Nisbett and his wife Dorothy had a 100-acre tract. It was probably on this tract that the first tavern was opened in Matawan. The 1704 minutes of the Court of Freehold recorded, "John Pearse and his wife and Lewis Nisbitt and his wife moved to have lizenses granted them keeping of Publick houses, which ye Court granted and ordered that they have them accordingly." Among her other activities while husband John Watson was away at sea, his socially prominent wife Hope Taylor kept an inn. Records of the Court of Sessions and Pleas, held at Freehold, July 23, 1745, show that Hope and several others petitioned to be allowed to be Public House Keepers. No one would have considered it unusual or unseemly for a person of her background and social position to maintain an inn. Many outstanding and respected men and women of the time engaged in the same business since, from the 1600s until the American Revolution, tavern keeping was regarded as "an honored means of livelihood."

Throughout the ages, geography has in large measure determined the routes of trade and travel. The importance of bays, rivers, creeks, and inlets in the history of transportation cannot be exaggerated, and nowhere is this more apparent than in New Jersey. Many streams that today are no more than winding brooks once carried a considerable commerce. In *From Indian Trail to Iron Horse,* Wheaton J. Lane wrote, "Of all the rivers in East New Jersey, the Raritan was by far the most important as a highway of commerce." With their access to the Raritan, it played an important part in the lives of the residents of Aberdeen and Matawan.

The trails of primitive man, those followed by the pack horses of the fur traders, the crude wagon of the early settler, the turnpike, the railway, even the course of the modern airplane were all mapped out in conformity with the lay of the land. Although originally only 2 to 3 feet wide, considerable portions of the Minisink trail later became roads and consequently exerted influences on travel and settlement. The quality of the roads varied dramatically according to Peter Kalm in *Travels in North America, 1748–1851.* He describes not only the effect the differences of ground, such as clay or sand, had on the quality of roads during the period, but also the workmanship:

> The people are likewise very careless in mending them. If a rivulet be not very great, they do not make a bridge over it, and travelers may do as well as they can to get over. Therefore many people are in danger of being drowned in such places, where the water is risen by a heavy rain.

From colonial times to the 1920s, water was a major mode of transportation. This image from 1907 shows a view of Matawan Creek from the railroad trestle.

Lane describes how the early roads were maintained by local labor. For the period between 1716 and 1760, townspeople were summoned to repair the roads. Each person who did not appear or provide a substitute was to be fined 4 shillings 6 pence for each day's missed service. Due to the poor quality of the work, the law was amended in 1760 so that the overseers and surveyors were now elected by the voters, rather than being appointed by the justice of the peace. All during the colonial period, up until 1800, farmers and town dwellers alike continued to be called out at intervals for the purpose of "keeping the roads in repair." It was not until 1804 that the overseers were required to keep a book recording the amount of labor expended by the inhabitants on the roads.

The problem of road quality continued for many years, as evidenced by the "Local Miscellany" column of the April 10, 1875 issue of *The Matawan Journal*, which read, "Some places, on the road leading from Matawan to Cartan's water-power mill, are in a miserable condition. We hope that the overseer of that district will touch up those spots next." The road being referred to was modern-day Church Street. Local Matawan lawyer John P. Applegate wrote an 1887 letter to his uncle about problems with the overseer arrangement. In it, he writes about hearing many complaints of how the road money needed to be expended on the roads "instead of going in the overseers pocket." Each overseer was allowed either $3 or $3.50 per each day's work with his team. Another complaint was that "they won't let you work your taxes out on the road any more; for that is deducted from the appropriation and leaves less for them; so the man who owns a farm pays his

Before the modern system of asphalt and concrete highways, overseers were responsible for road maintenance. Entries in a 1928 overseers log included $8 for one team for a day's scraping or carting gravel, and $3.50 for one team for a day carting cinders. This postcard shows Ravine Drive in the early twentieth century.

road tax, and the overseer puts it in his pocket." He explained that the township raised $8,000 per year for roads, and every spring, overseers were appointed and money apportioned at the rate of $63 per mile to each district. Applegate concluded his letter with the comment, "The office of overseer has gotten to be a salaried office, and there is as much a struggle for it as a presidential election, because if his appropriation is $500, $350 goes in his pocket and $150 on the roads."

Steen's comment that "it is not at all times easy to fix the location of those early Scotch settlers" will be echoed by many future historians as they attempt to determine locations and times of the various Presbyterian churches. Tradition is that between 1692 and 1705, the Scotch settlers worshipped in New Aberdeen, either in private homes or in a public meeting house. A public meeting house was not a church, but a building designated as the meeting place for the transaction of public business and the holding of secular and sacred activities.

Before 1692, worship was held in a log meeting house at a place near Wickatunk known to them as "Free Hill" and now known as Old Scots Burying Ground. It was in this log church in 1706 that the First Presbytery of the Presbyterian Church in America held its first recorded session. The list of Mt. Pleasant lot holders corresponds closely to the names found in early records of Old Scots Church. Graves of two of the original Mt. Pleasant lot holders, Richard Clark and Archibald Craig, are in the Old Scots Burying Ground. Three of the four men who moved the 1705 request for registration of the Free Hill meeting house were among the original landowners of New Aberdeen: Walter Ker, William Ronnol, and Patrick Imlay.

If the 1692 date for Old Tennent is accurate, the land for the church, at a spot called "White Hill," was donated by another Mt. Pleasant holder, John Reid. Ker was instrumental in the formation of both Old Scots and Tennent Churches. Per Woodrow's Scottish church records, Ker was banished from Scotland, leaving there in September 1685 at age 29 with his wife Margaret. Ker died June 10, 1742 at the age of 92. A marker at Old Tennent Church calls Ker the "Father of Old Tennent Church." Although some sources add a second "R" to Ker's name, the original spelling was probably with only one. Some of his descendants, including a Walter Kerr who dedicated the monument in the 1890s, chose the longer form. Charles Ker, who endowed a plaque in the walkway of Old Tennent Church in 1979, spelled the family name with one "R."

After Old Scots fell into disrepair and was abandoned in the 1730s, it would have been a long trip for Mt. Pleasant Presbyterians to go to Tennent Church. About 1760, a house of worship was erected in the old village of New Aberdeen. At first, the congregation at Middletown Point shared a pastor with Shrewsbury. The earliest deed for the Mt. Pleasant Church was from 1763, although there is some evidence that there may have been an earlier church there. The existence of a meeting house at Mt. Pleasant around 1734 is confirmed by an advertisement in the June 12, 1738 *New York Gazette*. Parties interested in renting a plantation in Middlesex County were advised to contact "James Mapces in Freehold, Monmouth County, near the Meeting House of James Rochead in Mt. Pleasant."

Several of the early Mt. Pleasant settlers were involved in the creation of other churches, including Walter Ker, who was among the founders of Old Scots Church. Gravestones at Old Scots provide additional clues about Matawan's early settlers. This is a rendering of Old Scots Church. (Courtesy of Old Tennent Presbyterian Church.)

There is a tradition that Rochead built the meeting house at his own expense after Old Tennent Church opened and Old Scots began to fall into disrepair.

The 1763 deed for 1.88 acres for the Mt. Pleasant church property was made to the Presbyterian Church of Monmouth County, and is supposed to include both the original church site and the cemetery. The property on New Brunswick Avenue, near Main Street, is described as follows:

> . . . a Certain Lott or Parcel of Land Situate Lying and Being in Middletown Aforesaid and Between Middletown Point and Mount Pleasant Beginning on a Course of North Fifty Nine Degrees West about Twelve Feet from a Large Stump Standing on the East Side of the Road that Goes from Mt. Pleasant to Middletown Point Thence Running First North Fifty Nine Degrees West Two Chains and Sixty Five links to a Stake Near a Red Oak Bush which said Red Oak Bush is marked on Four Sides. Then South Twenty Two Degrees West Five Chains and Seven Links to a Stake near to Two White Oak Bushes, Both Which Bushes are Marked on Four Sides, Thence North Seventy Three Degrees East Three Chains and Forty Three Links to the Highway Aforesaid, Thence North Twenty Two Degrees East Two Chains and Fifty Links to the Beginning Containing One Acre.

The Mt. Pleasant Cemetery adjoining the early church was used by the Presbyterian congregation until 1959. Samuel Forman was the grantor of the cemetery ground and several family members are buried there. Thirteen Revolutionary War veterans were buried at Mt. Pleasant. However, in the twentieth century, use of the cemetery declined severely and there were fewer than 24 burials made in that time period. The property fell into disrepair, and in 1978 the Presbyterian church deeded the cemetery to the borough, where it joined the Burrowes Mansion under the management of the Historic Sites Commission. In the 1980s, preservation work began at the cemetery, a number of fallen stones re-erected and broken ones repaired, the gravestones documented, and a picket fence built around the site.

As early as 1734, the Mt. Pleasant area had a doctor. The earliest physician in the vicinity was Dr. Peter LeConte, whose second wife was Valeriah, daughter of John Eaton, the founder of Eatontown, another Monmouth County town. Of Huguenot descent, LeConte was an elder in the Collegiate Church of Middletown Point and Shrewsbury and "preached as well as practiced," "giving his patients old school theology as well as allopathic doses." LeConte is buried in Mt. Pleasant Cemetery and his unique green-gray color stone is the earliest marker in the cemetery.

Many of the area's early settlers, including Dr. Peter LeConte, are buried at Mt. Pleasant Cemetery.

3. The Revolutionary War

For the last half of the eighteenth century, Middletown Point continued to develop. In 1756, it took three days to go by stage from New Jersey to Philadelphia. It is interesting to note that, although women did not receive the universal right to vote until the passage of the nineteenth Amendment in 1920, according to the *New Jersey Gazette Almanac and Year Book*, women voted in New Jersey from 1776 to 1807. The largest impact on the residents of both the town of Middletown Point and adjoining farms during this time was the colonies' impending fight for independence. Although only one general engagement, the Battle of Monmouth, occurred within Monmouth County, several militia fights of considerable magnitude did take place within the county. Added to this was the daily expectation, often realized, of raids by British regulars.

During the American Revolution, Middletown Point and its neighboring area was a center of activity. Both Middletown and Shrewsbury were known as "hotbeds of Tories." Some even took up arms against the rebels on behalf of the King. Many raids were made upon the Shrewsbury and Middletown Districts (of which modern-day Matawan and Aberdeen were a part), plundering, burning, and carrying off prisoners. The rich farms with their cattle, horses, sheep, hogs, and well-stocked cellars, smokehouses, and barns constantly attracted the Refugees from Sandy Hook and foraging parties from Staten Island. Many of the armed Tories were exiled Monmouthmen, who knew every secret of their former homes and used such knowledge to great advantage. The crews of the British transports and men-of-war in the Lower Bay, craving fresh provisions like chickens, milk, and butter after their long voyage across the ocean living on salt provisions, also wanted the products of the Monmouth farms.

Although the following description of the times from the *New Jersey Archives Second Series* refers to Bergen County, it could just as easily apply to Middletown Point and surrounding towns:

> Kidnappings, ambushes, and sundry thrilling escapades kept life from growing dull for such of the population as attempted to carry on the business of life in the no-man's land between royal and rebel spheres of control.

In *Early Dutch Settlers of Monmouth,* James Steen wrote, "no county in the State of New Jersey suffered more during the Revolution than did Monmouth, and in no county did the citizens respond more nobly. The proximity to the shore and readiness of access by boat from New York rendered it peculiarly the prey of the British." He describes the shooting of children and old men, hanging women, burning houses and barns, and destroying animals that could not be conveniently carried off.

A network of 23 signal towers was to be built throughout the state as part of a warning system to be lit if the enemy was sighted. The blazing fires would be the signals for the local militias to assemble. Instructions from Major General Dickinson for building the beacons directed that, "These fires should be made of logs intermixed with brush square at the bottom about sixteen feet and to diminish as they rise like a pyramid, and should be 18 to 20 feet high." A list of initial beacon locations, several of which were to be built in Monmouth County, was included in the *Writings of Washington,* a 31-volume set of books done for the bicentennial of George Washington's birthday. Beacons were supposed to have been built upon Center Hill in Monmouth, on Highlands Navesink, on Middletown Hill, and at Mt. Pleasant. Although not included in the official list of beacons, according to local lore, Fox Hill in Matawan, now the site of the Rose Hill Cemetery, was used as a vantage point for patriots to spy on British ships. Before houses were built, a person standing at the top of the hill could see the Raritan Bay and New York.

Not all the actions in the Middletown Point area were for the cause of independence. Leonard Lundin described the dichotomy of feelings in New Jersey during the Revolutionary War in *Cockpit of the Revolution: The War for Independence in New Jersey*:

Although a sketch of 1845 Matawan, it is reminiscent of the small 1700s village that served as the shipping port for the area. (Sketch by John W. Barber and Henry Howe, Historical Collections of the State of New Jersey.)

It was not only in Bergen that shrewd traders succeeded in eluding the vigilance of the American authorities and smuggling supplies into the welcoming arms of the British. According to common report, quantities of provisions found their way to the enemy from Shrewsbury, Middletown Point and Perth Amboy.

Among the important local figures during the colonial period were the Reverend Charles D. McKnight, John "Corn King" Burrowes, Major John Burrowes, and Philip Morin Freneau, who earned the title of "Poet of the Revolution" due to his patriotic writings. One of the oldest and still operating establishments in the town of Matawan is the Poets Inn, named in honor of Freneau, who lived nearby. Located on Route 79, the building was erected in the mid-1700s and has had many names, including the Mt. Pleasant Hotel, Dickson's Green Pump Inn, Freneau Hotel, and the Matawan Hotel. The building once served as a polling place, and at one time the local "tax collector" had his office in the lobby.

The first Burrowes came to the colonies during the seventeenth century for the same reason so many others fled England during that period—to escape religious persecution. Eden Burrowes moved from Long Island to Monmouth County and

When Benjamin F.S. Brown purchased the Burrowes Mansion at 94 Main Street in 1904, it was illuminated by gas lights and heated by fireplaces and stoves, including a coal stove in the kitchen.

established a plantation on Chapel Hill Road near Middletown Village. His son John was an established merchant by the time he was in his 20s. In partnership with Captain John Watson, the two men operated from Middletown Point. After Watson's death, Burrowes married his former partner's widow. He acquired a new partner, Samuel Forman. Forman, another wealthy merchant who owned mills, sloops, and a store in Middletown Point, was a member of one of the major families in Monmouth County. Samuel Forman and his wife, the former Helena Denise, lived at the corner of what is now Ravine Drive and Wyckoff Street, and their home was a social center of the village. Other Burrowes' partners included Peter Imlay and Richard Hartshorne.

There is some discrepancy about when the house at 94 Main Street was built that Burrowes was supposed to have purchased in 1769 and which was prominently featured in a skirmish during the Revolutionary War. John E. Stillwell in *Historical and Genealogical Miscellany, Volume 3* and local lore give the date of 1723 for the building of the house by John Bowne III. This is also the date used by Mary Lou Koegler in her book *The Burrowes Mansion of Matawan, New Jersey and Notations on Monmouth County History*. However, more recent archeological and cultural investigations date the building to the 1750s. According to Gail Hunton, principal historic preservation specialist with the Monmouth County Park System, the Georgian architecture did not come into use in the county until 1750. The lack of artifacts from the earlier time period recovered in digs at the mansion also helps substantiate the later date. The Burrowes Mansion passed from the hands of anyone who was in any way related to the Burrowes family on April 28, 1795, when Sheriff David Forman and his wife Anne deeded the mansion property to John I. Holmes for £5,000. Unfortunately, Holmes did not enjoy the property for long as it was seized from his estate and sold to Chrineyonce Van Mater of Middletown Township for £2,013 on March 17, 1800.

At the beginning of the American Revolution, John Burrowes was dealing primarily in corn. When it became a staple of the war, Burrowes became the major supplier. His prosperity earned him the nickname "Corn King Burrowes," and gave those who already disliked him for his politics reason to envy him. Even before war was officially declared, Burrowes had already determined his affiliation toward the fight for independence and was a member of the Sons of Liberty from 1765 to 1766. In 1774, he was a delegate to the Provincial Congress to choose the delegates to attend the Continental Congress, where independence for the colonies would be decided. Asher Holmes, another prominent Monmouth County patriot, was married to Sarah Watson, one of John Burrowes's stepdaughters.

Not all Burrowes's actions involved meetings and politics. He was also known to take more direct action. After the December 16, 1773 Boston Tea Party, a request went out for food and funds for the residences of that town. Local Monmouth County residents were to deliver donations of grain or money to Abraham Hendricks in Imlay's Town or Robert Rhea in Allen's Town. Burrowes offered the use of his sloop to transport contributions to Massachusetts. According to Larry R. Gerlach in *Prologue to Independence: New Jersey in the Coming of the American*

Revolution, in October 1775, the Bostonians received 14 bushels of rye and 50 bushels of rye meal from Monmouth. At a time when every Monmouth citizen who put his name on the militia role, or who identified himself with the cause of freedom, did so in the full knowledge that from that moment on his life was in constant danger, Burrowes permitted the first militia in the area to train in his front yard. His home is said to have served as a point of operations in General David Forman's network.

John Burrowes Jr., son of "Corn King," was a target of British loyalists and regulars both because of his father's actions and politics and his own. Sometime between 1776 and 1778, John Burrowes Jr. married Margaret Forman, daughter of his father's partner and cousin to General David Forman, who became one of the foremost figures of the revolution in Monmouth County. Forman was a great friend of George Washington and the mastermind of a coastal network for spying on British shipping and for reporting movements to the congress in Philadelphia. Forman had been nicknamed "Black David" to distinguish him from his cousin, Sheriff David Forman. Young Burrowes, who worked very closely with the general, was an officer in Forman's regiment of the Continental Army and was called "Black David's Devil" by those who hated them both.

Early in the war, the then Captain Burrowes (later Major) and Jonathan Forman, his wife's brother who had left Princeton to join the army, organized and trained a company of soldiers on the front yard of the Burrowes Mansion. Tradition has it that the mansion was also the point of departure for the "six months soldiers" (so named because half a year was to have been their period of enlistment), who marched away from Middletown Point to the tune of "Duncan Darie" on their way to join Washington's Continental Army. Jonathan Forman, who was a colonel in the revolution, also commanded the New Jersey regiment to put down the whiskey rebellion in Pennsylvania.

When the war began escalating, Burrowes moved his bride back to the mansion where he would spend every furlough. The secret visits did not go unnoticed for long. Hope Taylor Burrowes had many relatives in Middletown who were Tories: among them former sheriff John Taylor; Colonel George Taylor, who had served with the Monmouth Militia, but had deserted to the British; and the prominent loyalist leader William Taylor.

On May 27, 1778, Burrowes was sighted at his father's house and an attempt was made to capture him. A contingent of about 70 Skinner's Greens from Sandy Hook landed near Major Kearney's, crossed the mill-creek, and marched toward Burrowes's home. The attacking forces, now supplemented by local Tories, were seen and an alarm sent to Middletown Point and the Burrowes family. Members of the small local militia assembled somewhere near the center of town while other armed men joined Major Thomas Hunn's (Freneau) company. When the British forces came around the head of the Burrowes millpond at a point near present-day Church Street, they found themselves between two colonial fighting units. While the main British contingent dealt with the colonial forces or set mills, stores, and boats afire, a small fast-moving detachment went ahead to capture

Howard Henderson and Kimberly Meggison Bernath recreate the confrontation between a Loyalist soldier and Mrs. John Burrowes during the 1778 attempted capture of her husband, Captain John Burrowes, at the Matawan Tricentennial Parade in 1986.

young Burrowes. Mary Lou Koegler in *The Burrowes Mansion of Matawan, New Jersey* wrote, "mills, boats, storehouses and other buildings were ablaze throughout Middletown Point. It was said that the smoke could be seen for miles, and the stench of burning wood, clothing, and produce lingered for days."

When the British forces arrived at the Burrowes home, tradition has it that young Burrowes had already left through a back window, swum the creek, and hidden on the other side. Extracts from David Forman's handwritten manuscript illustrate the closeness of Burrowes's escape. It states, "that in his haste he left one boot behind" and that Burrowes hid himself for two days and a night without food in the dense woods to escape detection. There is also another part of the story. Clutching a shawl over her nightdress, Margaret Burrowes is reputed to have confronted the Tories. According to tradition, when ordered to turn over her shawl to bind the wound of an injured soldier, she is reputed to have clutched the garment more closely around her and replied, "You'll not get my shawl or anything else here to aid a British subject." The British officer then struck her

The restored Burrowes Mansion is the backdrop as the 1778 skirmish and attempted capture of Captain John Burrowes is reenacted as part of the activities celebrating the 300th anniversary of Matawan's founding.

with the hilt of his sword. The British soldiers then looted the house, and took most of the furniture outside and burned it. During modern renovations, scorch marks on the underside of some of the shingles led some to theorize that an attempt was made to burn the house also. The June 3 issue of *The New Jersey Gazette* reported that Burrowes Sr. was taken prisoner by the invading forces, who also burnt his mills and both his storehouses.

During the skirmish, Lieutenant Colonel Smock, Captain Christopher Little, Joseph Wall, and Captain Joseph Covenhoven were captured. Several people were killed, including Messrs Pearce and Van Brockle. The local loyalists returned to their homes and the majority of troops rowed back to Sandy Hook, while one group of Greens took Burrowes Sr. and the other captives to a prison on Staten Island. Colonel Thomas Henderson, Burrowes's son-in-law, organized a group of men and captured William Taylor of Middletown, who was eventually exchanged for the elder Burrowes. Burrowes survived his captivity and died in 1785. Margaret Burrowes survived the blow received in the skirmish. Although she bore two children between then and the time of her death in 1787, it was said that she was ill much of the time thereafter. Margaret was buried in Mt. Pleasant Cemetery at the age of 28 years, 11 months, and 16 days.

The other skirmish of note in Middletown Point involved the Presbyterian Church and its pastor the Reverend Charles D. McKnight. Ordained in 1741, McKnight was installed on October 16, 1744 as pastor of the Presbyterian congregations at Cranbury and Allen's Town. Anti-British sentiments were not something McKnight became acquainted with while at Matawan. In 1756, he was forced to resign as pastor at the Allen's Town Presbyterian Church when he tried to hold a conservative course within the church during the anti-British fervor growing within the town. McKnight accepted the call in April 1767 to provide pastoral services to Shrewsbury, Shark River, and Middletown Point. While at Middletown Point, McKnight's activities were less conservative. Historian William S. Hornor wrote that before and soon after the start of the revolution, the Mt. Pleasant church and its green were being used regularly for patriotic meetings—meetings fully supported by its pastor. During the January 1777 Battle of Princeton, McKnight served as chaplain to Continental troops.

Later that year in June, McKnight was involved in a skirmish at the Mt. Pleasant church during which men on both sides were killed or wounded. While visiting the church, a party of British troops led by a Lieutenant Moody attacked the place, burned the church, and took the pastor and others prisoner. They were taken to New York and confined in a prison ship, where McKnight was kept for some time. Church records from August 31, 1820 state the following:

> During the time of the American Revolution, when the Provinces were struggling to shake off the falling yoke imposed on them by Great Britain, and to establish a free & independent Government, which objects were at length happily accomplished. . . . The Church, in this place [Mt. Pleasant] under Pastoral care of the Rev. Charles McKnight, was burned, their Shepherd was imprisoned by the enemy, and shortly after his liberation, died.

McKnight died on January 1, 1778. After destruction of the church by the Tories, 21 years were to pass before another church building was erected on the site. A $1,500 lottery was authorized in 1793 for the purpose of raising funds to rebuild the church at Mt. Pleasant and a second church building was finally raised in 1798.

The skirmishes at the Burrowes Mansion and the Mt. Pleasant Church were not the only fighting seen by local men. In late May 1779, Middletown Point was attacked and a fight took place at the foot of the hill near Samuel Forman's home. The wounded were taken to Forman's home, which eventually became known as The Old Hospital. In an 1876 address, Judge William Spader tells of another skirmish when Peter Schenck "fled for his life when a party of British marauders were plundering and committing other acts of violence, besides burning the mill which stood near what is now called the red storehouse of Fountain, Hornor, & Company." Prior to the British occupation of New York, Captain Jacob Conover of Middletown was sent to Sandy Hook where he smashed the lamps of the lighthouse to prevent the expected British fleet from having the benefit of the same. He was afterwards taken prisoner at Middletown Point, brought on board one of the enemy vessels, and threatened to be hanged from the yardarm as a rebel. He was subsequently confined among the prisoners in the Sugar House in New York City. The military record of Thomas Geran shows that he enlisted in April 1780 as a sailor on a privateer, the cutter *Marque Rebecca*, under the command of Captain John Burrowes. Walter P. Hyer, son of an early township landowner, was injured in the 1781 Battle of Pleasant Valley.

Since volumes have been written about the Battle of Monmouth, only a brief mention will be made of the events that took place in present-day Manalapan on June 28, 1778. Among the local participants on the field of battle that day were John Burrowes Jr., Asher Holmes, and Thomas Henderson. The trio had also fought in the Battles of Germantown and Princeton in 1777, as well as in many of the local confrontations of the war. Although the Battle of Monmouth has been called the last major confrontation of the revolution in the North, Tory raids, naval warfare, and general fighting continued throughout the war. According to Koegler, "The Tories, realizing the war was gradually being won by the Americans, vented their frustrations by constantly raiding farms and towns, foraging for provisions, and creating havoc whenever possible throughout the area, including Middletown Point."

Unlike later military unit designations, during the Revolutionary War and the War of 1812, the units were named after the men who raised the money to outfit them. Later unit designations would be more descriptive, such as the 155th Depot Brigade in which Herman Lamberson served in World War I or the 1060th Base Unit of the United States Army Air Corps in which William Hubbs served in World War II. Both men were buried in Mt. Pleasant Cemetery. Among the Revolutionary War units, local men who are buried in Mt. Pleasant Cemetery served in Forman's Battalion of the Second New Jersey Regiment, Carhart's Company of the New Jersey State Troops, and Stillwell's New Jersey Regiment. In the First New Jersey Regiment were Forman's Company, Carhart's Company, Hunn's Company, and Scudder's Battalion. Local veterans of the War of 1812 served in the Middletown Point Militia, J. TenEyck's Rifles (a Middletown Point unit), and William TenEyck's Rifles (a Freehold unit).

A large number of Monmouth County Tories went into British service as members of the New Jersey Royal Volunteers, commonly known as "Skinner's Greens," taking their name from their commander General Courtland Skinner and the distinctive color of their uniform. Skinner was a lawyer who had been the royal attorney of New Jersey when he was commissioned by General Howe, head of the British forces, to raise an army to be based at Sandy Hook. Most of the men who enlisted with Skinner did so out of true belief in Britain's sovereignty.

Other local men fought not on land, but in the whaleboat navy. Unlike later wars on American soil, the Revolutionary War was to a large extent a coastal war. The sea was often the main supply source of materials for the occupying armies. The traffic, so close to shore, was susceptible to surprise by swift-rowing whaleboats dashing out of the night. The technique was heavily practiced in the waters around New York where the greatest mass of shipping clustered and where, as a consequence, the greatest riches lay. Local men captured British vessels and privateers and brought them into Matawan Creek to lie until disposed of by the Admiralty court of which Major John Burrowes was named marshall in late 1780. Hornor wrote in a 1936 *Matawan Journal* article that at one time during 1780, two sloops and a schooner were tied up at the docks.

Designed for the shallow waters between Matawan and Sandy Hook, the whaleboats were built for tidewater operation by tidewater men. The 26- to 30-foot-long, light wooden vessels were propelled by leather-muffled oars. Broad of beam and shallow of draft, the ships were by design pointed at both ends, so they could quickly reverse direction. Each vessel was crewed by 14 to 24 tightly disciplined, experienced seamen armed with boat hooks, grapnels, and hand or duck guns. The men had muskets or long duck guns, but the chief weapons were pistols and cutlasses. Unlike the larger naval vessels that carried cannons, the whaleboats' only artillery was a small swivel gun (in reality a large-sized musket) mounted at bow or stern of the largest boats.

The smallest of the three contingents of the whaleboat navy was based in Middletown Point. Depending on the source, between two to six boats made

This Ravine Drive residence, the Forman House, is one of the earliest buildings in the area. It is known as the "Old Hospital," obtaining its name after being used as a field hospital after a Revolutionary War skirmish. This photograph was taken in 1936.

their hiding place in the ravines branching off from Matawan Creek. The mill stream (Gravel Brook) had been widened and deepened below the mill dam so that a vessel of 100 tons could berth beside the mills on the creek. Corn King Burrowes also allowed his mill pond to be used as one of the hiding places for the Middletown Point whaleboat navy. When not in use, the boats were tucked away along Matawan Creek and its tributaries. According to Koegler, at least one vessel was always kept at the head of Burrowes's pond.

Among the various whaleboat actions was the June 1777 taking of prisoners in New York by Captain William Marriner, a New Brunswick tavern keeper. In *Where the Raritan Flows*, Earl Schenck Miers describes Marriner as "one of the foremost of those hardy whaleboatmen." Having decided that too many New Jersey patriots were being held prisoner in the holds of British vessels, Marriner and Captain John Schenck of the local militia undertook a mission into the heart of British territory to obtain suitable prisoners to exchange. Fred J. Cook commented in *What Manner of Men* that Schenck knew the region around Flatbush, New York well as his family had relatives there whom he had visited since boyhood. Marriner and Schenck drew up a list of prominent Tories whom they hoped to capture, including David Matthews, the Tory mayor of New York; Miles Sherbrook, a personal foe of Marriner; the wealthy Jacob Suydam; Colonel Axtell; and Theophylact Bache, president of the New York Chamber of Commerce, whose brother Richard had married a daughter of Benjamin Franklin.

With Schenck and Marriner went 26 picked men in two whaleboats. They set out from Matawan Creek on the southwestern shore of Raritan Bay as soon as

The twentieth-century boating industry in Matawan and Aberdeen is significantly different from that of the eighteenth century. In this 1950s image, private boats in marinas have replaced the whaleboats, schooners, and sloops of yesteryear. (Courtesy of Dina and Louis Zampelle.)

night fell and they hugged the dark shoreline so that their boats would blend in with the land and escape observation by British patrols on the bay. Leaving the regular crew in the boat ready for an instant take-off, Marriner and Schenck made their way to Matthews's home in Flatbush with ten men. Fortunately for him, he had chosen that night to be out. Going next to a neighboring house, the invaders from New Jersey released an American prisoner billeted there, Captain Alexander Graydon. At other houses, the whaleboatmen captured Bache and Moncrief, a British major. Illustrating the speed of the small boats, especially when lifted along by a storm, the whaleboatmen reached Keyport in the incredible time of an hour and a quarter. Docking at Matawan before 6 a.m., they sent their captives on horseback to General Washington at Morristown, and by the end of July, both had been exchanged for American prisoners.

The Revolutionary War was not the only action in the town. As a seaport, Middletown Point must have had its share of thieves and brigands. Koegler wrote the following in *The Burrowes Mansion of Matawan, New Jersey*:

> There is a record of a counterfeiter who set up business in town in 1773
> in conjunction with cohorts in Perth Amboy who all passed themselves
> off as silversmiths while actually making bogus coins.

Another incident involving Burrowes Sr. has been recorded in the *New Jersey Archives*. In 1774, the Burrowes store was robbed and he utilized the newspapers to advertise the event. Reading an account of the theft in *The New Jersey Gazette* issue of September 14, 1774, it is interesting to see what items were popular at the time. Stolen were assorted fabrics, including one piece rich black satin, one piece black peelong, one piece three-quarters of a yard wide and one piece of yard-wide black mode, one piece of black spotted peelong, two remnants blue peelong, one piece black sarsanet, 2 or 3 yards fine flowered lawn, 3 yards broad striped muslin, three pieces fine callicoes, and one piece green lutestring. Among the handkerchiefs stolen were nine or ten crossbar'd Kenting handkerchiefs, three dozen plain striped border'd, one dozen flowered, nine or ten crossbar'd red and white cotton handerkerchiefs, and blue and white spotted handkerchiefs. Also stolen was six pair of cypher'd sleeve buttons, set in silver; one piece minionet; and about £7 in cash. The article also stated the following:

> It is hoped that all persons will do their endeavor to discover the robbers.
> Ten pounds reward will be given to any person for apprehending the
> robber or robbers, to be paid on conviction, and the tenth part of the
> goods recovered, by Henry Remsen in New York, or by the subscriber
> at Middletown Point.

The theft at Burrowes's store was not the only one in Matawan's history. In 1896, Fritz Gelenius, who kept a grocery store near Matawan, was found dead in the cellar of his store on Sunday morning with his head battered. One of his pockets was turned inside out and the cash drawer was rifled of its contents. The supposition is that the murderer went into the store and asked for a glass of cider, then followed Gelenius when he went down to get it. A glass with some cider in it was near the body. In the spring of 1921, four clerks at A.J. Cartan's store at Matawan were held up and the day's receipts of several hundred dollars were stolen.

The wooden building with the fancy gingerbread, steep roof, and starburst at the peak was the town's early post office. In 1897, Benjamin F.S. Brown was not only postmaster thereof; he was also owner of the Matawan Journal, *which published such news as the Fritz Gelenius murder.*

4. OF TOWN AND FIELD

In the nineteenth century with the War for Independence over, the United States began to settle the problems involved in simply existing as a new nation and producing its own goods for consumption, such as textiles for clothing, machinery for farming, and vehicles for transportation. From its earliest beginnings, the American people were primarily agricultural, but during these years, manufacturing and transportation took firm root in the nation. The Matawan-Aberdeen area was no exception, as industry joined agriculture in the region. Other significant events and impacts on the area were the Civil War in the 1860s and the burgeoning social movements. A post office was not established in town until 1815 with Cornelius P. Vanderhoof as the first postmaster, although the area did have some mail service as far back as 1795 when Jonathan Forman was postman. A post office was established in 1889 in Freneau with Milton A. Fardon as the first postmaster, but service was discontinued in the summer of 1925. The Cliffwood Post Office was established in 1885.

Among the political changes during the first seven decades of the nineteenth century was the creation of Matawan Township as an entity. The first subdivision of Monmouth County occurred in 1693 with the creation of the townships of Middletown, Shrewsbury, and Freehold. What was to become Matawan and Aberdeen was then part of Middletown Township and would remain so until 1848 when Raritan Township (which was to include the Matawans) was formed. Less than ten years later, in 1857, Raritan Township would be split and Matavan Township—including the village of Middletown Point—was formed. Reverting to the name by which its creek was originally known to early settlers, the township changed its name to Matawan in 1882.

Because of confusion with Middletown Township, it became necessary in 1865 to change the name of Middletown Point to Matawan Village. The Borough of Matawan was created as a separate entity from the township in 1885 under the Commission Act. When the borough was created, the limits were described as follows:

> Beginning at the dock of the propeller S.S. Wyckoff on the Matawan
> Creek; thence easterly to what is known as the Africa Road, and

following said road to the first overhead bridge on the F. & N.Y. [Freehold and New York] Railway; thence southerly along the said railway to the Mt. Pleasant Station; thence westerly along the centre of the road leading to the Old Bridge Turnpike; and along the turnpike to Matawan Creek; thence northerly following current of said creek to the place of beginning at the propeller dock.

In 1896, the commission form of government was changed, and the borough was reorganized as a mayor and council form of government—the form it continues to use today.

John W. Barber and Henry Howe described the Matawan-Aberdeen area in 1844 as follows:

> The village of Middletown Point is upon a narrow point of land formed by two branches of the Matteawan Creek, 3 m. from Raritan bay, and 12 from Freehold. It was early settled by Scotch and called New Aberdeen.

The village was described as a thriving business place with a bank, 11 stores, 25 mechanic shops, and about 80 dwellings, "many of them large and commodious." A steamer plied between it and New York. The 1834 *Gazetteer of the State of New Jersey* also mentioned four taverns and a grist mill; "This is the market of an extensive country, and large quantities of pork, rye, corn, cord wood, and garden truck, are thense sent to New York." Middletown Point and Mt. Pleasant were listed as the villages.

The lifestyle in the Matawans in the early part of the nineteenth century was very different than today's. Merchants still wrote their letters with quill pens and used sand to dry the ink. There were no street letterboxes; letters had to be carried to the post office. It cost 18¢ to send a letter from Boston to New York. A day laborer earned two shillings a day. Stoves were unknown; all cooking was done at an open fireplace. Beef, pork, salt fish, potatoes, and hominy were staples of diet all year round. Among the technological advances to come to Matawan in the 1870s were the telegraph and a new illuminant, gas. The kerosene lights, which had replaced the candles and whale oil lamps of colonial days, were themselves being replaced. William Arose, sexton of the Rose Hill Cemetery, noted in 1874 that "in the 19 years he had been there over 1,000 people had been buried with two-thirds under the age of 20."

Through his entries in his diaries, Charles Wardell, who resided for many years at 198 Main Street, provides an insight into this different era. Wardell, who was hired by the Farmers and Merchants Bank shortly after coming home from service in the Civil War, became cashier in 1873 and remained at his post for over 40 years. Many of the social activities Wardell wrote about were centered around religious and civic organizations. Often the meetings concerned current events, such as his diary entry of Wednesday, February 24, 1869 on the Matawan Literary

Society meeting in the Odd Fellows Hall. The evening's activity was a debate on whether or not women should have the right to vote.

Sledding and ice skating on the local ponds were popular pastimes during the winter months. In *The Burrowes Mansion of Matawan, New Jersey,* Mrs. Edwin H. Dominick tells that winter sleighing parties held on the hill outside of the Forman House (Ravine Drive) in the 1700s were especially popular. The practice of sledding on the Ravine Drive hill, which was also known as Carriage Factory Hill, continued well into the twentieth century. That is not to say that this bucolic life was without novelty and excitement. One example of an extraordinary event was Wardell's entry for Sunday, August 10, 1884, which simply read, "earthquake 2.05 p.m."

Unlike today's modern age where many people obtain their news through electronic media such as television, radio, and the Internet, in the nineteenth century, newspapers provided both local and national news. Although no longer in publication, *The Matawan Journal* was at one time the town's local paper, but it was not the only one. The first newspaper published in the vicinity was the *New Jersey Chronicle*, published by Philip Freneau in 1795. Another early paper was the *Workmen's Advocate* started by George H. Evans in 1830. Edgar Hoyt's *Middletown Point Union* was published for about two years in the mid-1840s. George C. Waite started *The Democratic Banner & Monmouth Advertiser* in 1848 before selling it three years later to George W. Bell and Charles W. Fountain. They sold it the following year to Henry Morford, who changed the name to *New Jersey Standard*.

In the early 1850s, Edmund O'Brien started the short-lived *Atlantic and Monmouth County Advertiser*. Jacob R. Schenck purchased the press and material

Winter entertainments in the nineteenth and early twentieth centuries were sledding, sleigh riding, and ice skating, and the tradition continued for many years. Prince took the family to town by sleigh in 1940. (Courtesy of Marie Dietrich Busch.)

Both Rose Street and Rose Hill Cemetery were named after Joseph Rose, who lived in this mansion on County Road in Cliffwood, opposite Rose Street. (Courtesy of the Aberdeen Township Historical Commission.)

and published the *New Jersey Weekly Times: Middletown Point and Keyport Advertiser*. The paper, which was started in 1857, had to cease operations during the Civil War while its editor served in the Union army as quartermaster of the 29th New Jersey Regiment of Volunteers. A November 1862 letter in Jim Stephen's history of the 29th recorded the following:

> One of the happiest men in the regiment is Jacob R. Schenck, former editor of the *Middletown Point Times* and I am pleased to say, that courteous, obliging and jovial, he is one of the regimental favorites. He is supported in his labors by the same untiring energy that enabled him to live respectably for five years from the income of a printing office that issued 550 papers a week and furnished the town with its handbills at the lowest charges, with editorial puffs gratuitously bestowed. He is in excellent spirits and health.

What was to be the local source for news of the state, nation, and local area, *The Matawan Journal*, began in the summer of 1869. Originally *The Journal and Matawan Advertiser*, David A. Bell started the paper in a room over the drugstore belonging to his brother George Bell. A year later, the paper was changed from a monthly to a bi-weekly. The following year, it was enlarged to 24 columns and made a weekly selling for $1 a year. Benjamin F.S. Brown acquired the paper and became its editor in 1890, establishing a publishing dynasty that was to last well into the next century. After Brown's death in the summer of 1920, the family kept the award-winning paper going as his daughter J. Mabel Brown took over editorial responsibilities. *The Matawan Journal* and its sister paper *The Keyport Weekly* were sold in December 1971 to Shore Publishers, Inc., which closed them down two years later when the parent company went bankrupt.

Local bands entertained the residents until just after the beginning of the twentieth century. The Matawan Cornet Band was organized in 1884 and the Citizen's Brass Band two years later. The Cornet Band played at a skating rink it built on what would later become the site of the Second Baptist Church. Among the events the brass band played at was the 1892 Columbian Celebration in New York City. In 1894, the two bands joined together to form the Matawan Brass Band of 20 members and played until 1906. In addition to local concerts, the group played in Philadelphia, Trenton, and Newark, and at the 1900 Theodore Roosevelt parade in New York City. In the early 1900s, the group performed a series of ten open-air concerts per season in front of the carriage factory at the corner of Ravine Drive and Main Street. The concerts were paid for by public subscriptions amounting to $500.

Rose Hill Cemetery, named not for the flower but for Joseph Rose who once owned the land, was established in 1858 on land purchased from James Fountain. Joseph Rose came to Cliffwood from New York City after having served in the New York State Assembly, as well as being a city official responsible for the purchase of Central Park. He served on the Matawan Township Committee and on the Monmouth County Board of Chosen Freeholders. He died in the 1870s and is buried at the cemetery named after him. Over the years, veterans from five wars, including the Civil War, Spanish-American War, and the Korean Conflict have been buried there. The uniqueness of Rose Hill is its topography. From the cemetery's highest point, the Raritan Bay and the skyline of New York City can be viewed. Local lore has it that the hill was a lookout area for the local Lenape tribe. Arrowheads and other evidence of Native American activity have been found at Rose Hill.

Matawan has the distinction of being the first town in Monmouth County to organize a volunteer fire company. When Washington Engine Company was organized in 1869, among the founding members were Jesse L. Sickels, William Maggs, and William Wiltberger. The three were active New York City firemen before moving to Matawan. The company purchased a lot for a firehouse from Mrs. Little for $200 and then purchased a hand-brake engine from the Guardian Engine Company No. 2 of the New York City Volunteer Company. The engine was transported by the *Steamboat Matteawan* to the dock at Keyport, where members picked it up. Washington Engine's firehouse was originally on Little Street (next to the present-day First Aid Squad building); then in 1976, a new firehouse was built on Jackson Street. This was not the first firehouse on

Jackson Street, as for many years after the turn of the century the Hook and Ladder Engine Company had a house for their equipment there. Seven years after its incorporation, Washington Engine, 45 men strong, responded to a fire in neighboring Keyport that damaged or destroyed much of the central part of town. After many years of faithful service, the engine was retired and placed in storage where it was, ironically, destroyed in a fire. There was an earlier attempt at organizing a fire company in 1836 when the legislature incorporated the Franklin Fire Engine Company of Middletown Point. There is no record, however, that Franklin Engine ever existed beyond paper.

The Hook and Ladder Company No. 1 was the second fire company in town. Originally named Phoenix, the company was organized in late 1877. Their first equipment was a secondhand truck purchased from a company in Hoboken, New Jersey. It arrived in Matawan by train on Thanksgiving Day, 1877, with free transportation arranged by Moses W. Stall, the ticket agent at the Matawan station. Judge William Spader originally furnished a building for them that the company used until they moved to the rear of the Borough Hall on Main Street. The firehouse was later used by the YMCA. The Hook and Ladder Company later built a firehouse on 161 Broad Street that it shares with the Midway Hose Company.

The first one-third of the nineteenth century was the turnpike era in America. Early turnpikes were built to connect New York City with Philadelphia and to provide outlets for farmers. For better maintenance, turnpikes were plank roads

In 1877, Washington Engine, 45 men strong, responded to a fire in neighboring Keyport that damaged or destroyed much of the central part of town, including two hotels, one church, and 25 other buildings. The "modern" engine pictured here, a 500-gallon-per-minute pumper, had more capabilities than the unit's earlier hand pumper.

Just as the pack mules of fur traders followed Lenape trails, cars now follow in the tracks of the mule or horse-drawn wagons of yesteryear. This image shows South Street, c. 1915.

consisting of one or two tracks, each 8 to 9 feet wide. The roadbed was 3 to 5 stringer boards buried lengthwise with 3-inch-thick planks laid crosswise on the road. A thin layer of sand or gravel covered the road to reduce wear and tear. The cost to build these roads was $1,800 per mile. The longest plank road in the area was constructed by the Monmouth County Plank Road Company beside the public road connecting Freehold and Keyport. Some years earlier, another officer at the bank, De Lafayette Schenck, was supposed to have been a moving spirit in getting the "nearly impossible" road to Freehold converted to a plank road and gravelled turnpike.Other plank roads were the Holmdel and Middletown Point Turnpike (which became Route 34 south of Main Street in Matawan), and the Middlesex and Monmouth Turnpike (which became Route 516). Companies were protected from travelers riding around tollgates on byways known as "shun pikes" by the imposition of penalties equal to a fine of three times the legal toll. Although tolls varied by turnpike, the following tolls charged by the Trenton and New Brunswick Turnpike were not far from average. Carriages were charged 1¢

55

A strong competition existed between Keyport boats and those of neighboring Middletown Point, often turning a normal passage into a thrilling race as rival captains called for every ounce of steam and the paddle wheelers furiously churned their way across New York's lower bay.

per mile for each horse up to four, with 2¢ per additional horse. Tolls per mile for a dozen calves, sheep, or hogs were half a cent or 1¢ for a dozen cattle, mules, or horses.

Significant progress was made in the transportation of goods and people during the 1800s as the canal boats of the early 1800s gave way to steam power. In 1807, roads between Matawan and New Brunswick were little more than footpaths impassable by horse and wagon. It took six days by stagecoach to travel between New York and Boston. Ellis describes sloops as the only mode of conveying people to New York City until the steamboats came. He also wrote that amusing stories are told of the trials the people underwent during the three to four day journey over to New York. Averaging only 4.5 miles per hour, the first steamboats were not as fast as stages, but had the thrill of the novelty of steam propulsion and were more pleasurable than riding over rough roads in hot and crowded wagons.

The mid-1800s have been called the great days of steam boating. Steamboats were not just confined to western rivers. *Steamboat to the Shore* by George H. Moss Jr. and *Steam Vessels Built In Old Monmouth 1841–1894* by Leon Reussille document the history of many of the boats that served Middletown Point during the heyday of the steamboat. In the 1820s, steamships traveling between Matawan and New York City brought summer visitors to the area. Farm trade provided the steamers' main cargo during the winter months when visitors stayed home. In later years, a short line train carried produce from Freehold through Matawan to the Keyport pier. The New York & Long Branch Railroad ended traditional dependence on steamboats to take out vegetables and to bring in summer visitors. Over the years, Cliffwood was a seasonal stop, until ice forced service to cease, for steamships running between New York and Keyport.

Fountain, Hornor and Company ran sloops to New York City from 1812 until business required greater transport capabilities. A meeting was held in 1834 to get a steamboat, but the group did not get one until 1837 when the following advertisement was issued:

> Capt. G. Hiers states that "the new low-pressure steamboat 'Monmouth' will run during the months of April and May from the foot of Robinson street, New York, to Middletown Point, touching at Seguine's Dock, Staten Island and Key Port. Fare to and from Middletown Point, 50 cents. On the arrival of the boat at Middletown Point a stage will leave for Monmouth Court-House." Stages also ran from Long Branch, Red Bank and Shrewsbury in connection with this boat.

In addition to Fountain, Hornor and Company, the Keyport and Middletown Point Steamboat Company also ran ships between Keyport, Middletown Point, and New York City.

Although steamboat travel was an improvement over earlier modes of transportation, entries in the Wardell diaries show that travel by steamboat could be hazardous to passengers. The diaries mention the *James Christopher* blowing a hole in her boiler while steaming from New York to Red Bank on December 12, 1856. That same year, his diary noted on June 2 that he went down to the pier in New York to meet the steamboat, but it hadn't arrived yet. It continued that the ship "lay aground in the river all day." On the ship's return trip from New York,

Later renamed the Monmouth County Agricultural Railway, the New York and Freehold Railway passed through the eastern section of the borough, crossing Lake Matawan on a trestle (photo c. 1953). (Courtesy of the North Jersey Electric Railway Historical Society.)

it got stuck in the ice and "remained all night atomb, 2 miles from Keyport." Even travel by sailing ship could be dangerous, as the local paper reported in 1871 that the schooner *Joseph I. Thompson*, "while beating down the Narrows on Wednesday, 30th, was capsized during a heavy squall." The article also reported that the captain and crew were picked up in an exhausted state, and the *Thompson* was righted by the Coast Wrecking Company and taken to Staten Island for repairs. The loss due to the capsizing was estimated at about $500.

The railroad came to Matawan in the summer of 1875 when the laying of a single track from South Amboy to Long Branch was completed. One piece of local lore is how the railroad came to Matawan rather than Keyport. William Little (a local merchant and officer of the Farmers and Merchants Bank) advised bank customers to buy up the stock of the Jersey Central Railroad at 10¢ per share. The story goes that Matawan residents bought more stock than Keyport residents, $100,000 as compared to $3,000, and got the railroad. People who had bought the Jersey Central stock at 10¢ a share were to see it go up to over $200 per share.

Although the charter for a second railway through Matawan was issued in 1867, due to the company going into receivership, it was not until ten years later that a connection was made between the east-west line and the north-south one. To celebrate the connection, a special train was run on July 2, 1877. Revenue service began the next day and it was also on July 3 that the name was changed to the Freehold and New York Railway Company. Passenger service from Freehold

The Freneau station was established in 1877 as the Mt. Pleasant Station, but was renamed to Freneau in 1890. Built in 1906, the station building was retired in 1955 and moved to Allaire State Park, where this picture was taken.

Cecila Jones Van Brunt was a matriarch of the Van Brunt family, who founded Van Brunt Trucking Company, acknowledged, in September 1985, as the oldest trucking firm in America. (Courtesy of the Bentley family.)

to Matawan was provided into the 1950s, while freight service continued into the 1970s.

The different means of transportation were not independent of each other. When the steamboat *Monmouth* started service between New York and Keyport in the late 1830s, several stage lines were organized to meet the ship, including the Matawan Stage Line. After a succession of owners, William L. Van Brunt acquired the business in 1889. Besides the freighting operations, the firm ran a "taxi" service to the railroad station and supplied carriages and horses for such events as weddings, holiday visits, and funerals. According to Harvey Van Brunt, son of the firm's founder, in a 1963 *Newark Sunday News* article, "We always had 35 or more horses on hand." Before the advent of the motor truck, one of Van Brunt's major freight customers was the Matawan Steel and Iron Company, and a local fire company used Van Brunt's horses to pull their equipment. Van Brunt and Son purchased its first truck, a Federal, in 1914 and began running produce from Monmouth County to New York City. During World War II, the firm was a principal carrier of military supplies manufactured in plants in New Jersey and Pennsylvania. After more than 75 years in town, the firm left Matawan in 1963 when a new terminal at Old Bridge replaced the old stables on Broad Street in Matawan.

Until the second half of the twentieth century, clay-based industries were of major importance in Matawan and Aberdeen. During America's formative years, stoneware vessels provided the jugs, jars, churns, and other utilitarian vessels

Van Schoick and Dunn jugs and crocks are known for their cobalt double flower. Some of the decorative designs on the firm's wares have been attributed to Ezra Dunn, who was listed in the 1850 census as a painter. Today, collectors recognize the pieces by the blue floral design.

needed by a growing country. Salt-glazed stoneware was one of the most common types of pottery used in early America. Among the early potteries in what was to become Matawan were G&W Hickman, John A. Campbell, and Richard Low in the 1830s, and the potteries of Abial Price and Thomas Cottrell in the 1840s. Price, a member of the well-known Price family of New Jersey potters, founded a pottery in Middletown Point about 1844. An advertisement of February 26, 1846 in the *Monmouth Democrat* announced that in addition to his manufacture of stove tubes, drain pipe, and stove linings, that Price had made arrangements for the production of stone, earthen, and crockery ware. Price's pottery was opposite the Union Hotel, which was located at or near the intersection of Main and Little Streets. The pottery was only in business for about eight years and ceased operation upon Price's death in early 1852. Water Street in Aberdeen Township was formerly known as Price Street after Price.

Later in the nineteenth century, the stoneware tradition continued in Middletown Point with the formation of the J.L. Rue Pottery on Main Street and the most well-known of the Matawan potteries, Van Schoick and Dunn.

The J.L. Rue Pottery Company started operations in 1881 with two kilns making earthenware, Rockingham ware, and yellowware. Unlike the other firms, J.L. Rue was known for molded, rather than thrown, pieces. In 1895, the firm went into receivership and the 3 acres of land, the buildings, and equipment were sold for $750.

Shortly after Price's death, Ezra Dunn and his partner Josiah Van Schoick, who had worked at Noah Furman's pottery in Cheesequake, rented Price's pottery and began manufacturing stoneware in Middletown Point. Van Schoick and Dunn moved operations in 1862 to Washington Street near Jackson Street. In *Early Makers of Handcrafted Earthenware and Stoneware in Central and Southern New Jersey*, M. Lelyn Branin wrote that in 1860, the Van Schoick and Dunn Pottery had a reported capital of $4,000 and employed seven men. All of the wares were thrown by hand, and the factory required $500 worth of clay and 300 cords of wood annually.

Charles E. Close described the pottery operations in *The Matawan Journal* of August 9, 1935 as being located just above the gully bridge:

> The firm manufactured stone and earthen ware, snuff jars and drain tile as well as flower pots. At that time they supplied all of Monmouth County and parts of Ocean County with the output of their factory. The supplies were loaded on a large covered wagon, which would take a day to get as far as Manasquan [N.J.] unloading as it traveled from place to place. After the last of the orders were delivered, the caravan would head home, taking two days and one night for the trip.

During the latter part of the 1860s, the firm was expanded to include another Middletown Point man, William A. Dunlap. During the 1870s, a brick manufacturing unit was added to the business. According to the firm's 1907 incorporation papers, when it took on the name of Dunlap and Lisk Pottery Company, the firm had ceased the manufacture of salt-glazed stoneware, but

In the 1800s, bricks made from clay dug out of Terhune Park were used to build several houses in town. This brick bridge carrying Main Street over Aberdeen Creek replaced a stone one. (Courtesy of the Monmouth County Park System.)

continued to make and sell drain and sewer pipe, flue linings, yellow ware, Rockingham ware, and flower pots. Although manufacturing operations ceased during the middle of the twentieth century, Dunlap and Lisk is still an active firm in Matawan at the time this book was written.

Matawan and Aberdeen had many other industries during the 1800s. In 1835, mercantile interests were confined to a general store opened that year by Thomas I. Bedle, father of Governor Joseph D. Bedle, and a lumberyard operated by Francis P. Simpson and Company. In 1846, Austin Reid and David Craig Company had a flourishing business manufacturing coaches and light carriages. An 1850 list of Matawan compiled at that time by Thomas A. Hurley shows other local business activities, including M. Burke, carriage maker; Daniel Carhart, blacksmith; Tunis Hubbard, saddle and harness maker; Mrs. M. Cook, fancy confectionary store proprietor; and Gordon D. White, tin and stove manufacturer. The Burrowes Mansion is noted on Lightfoot's 1851 Map of Monmouth County as "The Steamboat Hotel." During the inn phase, the upstairs bedrooms in the wing of the building were supposedly partitioned to make more rooms to accommodate a greater number of guests. The advertisement in the 1875 county directory for the Matawan House at 121 Main Street stated it had an attached livery.

The 1878 *Geological Survey of New Jersey Report on Clays* estimated that 18 million bricks were made yearly at brickyards in Matawan and neighboring Keyport.

From the area's settlement until the industrial era, many creeks had mills on them for milling grain, as well as other uses. This mill was on the Dietrich Church Street farm (c. 1892). (Courtesy of Marie Dietrich Busch.)

During the settlement and Colonial era, overshoot mills were common throughout the area for milling grain and other uses.

Among the manufacturers listed in the 1875 county directory were Jason Burrows, A. Vandeventer, Charles A. Shultz, and Daniel Denton. Brick making continued in the area for many years as evidenced by entries in the 1914 *Farm & Business Directory of Monmouth County*. The directory listed three brick manufacturers in Cliffwood and two in Matawan.

William D. Bailey established a mill in 1864 at the back of his hardware store on Main Street and Valley Drive (now Route 34). He also operated a sash and blind business there until his death in 1914. In 1909, in preparation for retirement, he went into partnership with his two sons-in-law Cliffword W. Hulsart and William S. Lisk. In 1922, the two remaining partners dissolved the partnership with Hulsart taking over the hardware store and Lisk the mill. In 1936, the firm was the third oldest industry in Matawan and was described as one of the "most widely known millwork plants in the state." Other mills in the area were the Union Steam Saw Mills and Excelsior Mills. In the spring of 1879, C.S. Bucklin and Company erected brick buildings and started a business of canning fruits and vegetables. The firm employed 125 people during the 1885 fruit season.

Among businesses listed or advertising in the *Monmouth County Directory for 1875* were: William M. Bogart, manufacturer of and dealer of sash, blinds, and doors on Main Street near Gulley Bridge; W.E. Arrowsmith, general furnishing undertaker advertised orders for funerals promptly attended to, day or night; and

Once a familiar sight in the triangle formed between Broad and Main Streets, Disanto's Shoe Shop (c. 1907) would eventually be the site of Memorial Park. (Courtesy of the DiSanto family.)

J. Truex, carriage manufacturer, on Main Street. William L. Terhune and Dayton & Taylor were the lawyers in town and George W. Bell, the druggist, had a store on Main Street opposite the hotel.

A variety of stores provided local residents with a range of wares from furniture to shoes. A.H. Harris operated a country store and Nelson Painton was listed as a green grocer. Fountain Hornor and Company also had a country store along with their freighting service. M.T. Bissell's furniture store was at the corner of Main and Spring Streets. The buildings of Cartan and Devlin lumber and coal yard were a fixture on Main Street until the 1960s when they were torn down to make way for an apartment complex. An 1852 advertisement for J. Lewis and Company, located next to E.H. Dayton's store, stated the following:

> offer to the public one of the very best assortments of Boots and Shoes, of all descriptions, ever kept in the County, which they are prepared to sell on very favorable terms, for Cash or Country produce. Men's Fine Boots from $2.50 to $5.00, Coarse Boots from $1.25 to $2.50, Ladies' Bushkins, Boots, Gaiters, Slippers, &c, from $0.38 to 1.75. Children's Shoes from $0.23 upwards.

Matawan was a major banking town for many years. In 1830, farmer De Lafayette Schenck and merchant William Little started the process of getting a bank in Middletown Point by petitioning the state to grant a charter for the

Farmers and Merchants Bank. According to Ellis, Schenck was the first American child named after the Marquis de Lafayette. Little and Schenck advertised their intention in newspapers; anyone who wished to object to the legislation could do so. Over a year after the process of getting subscribers for the $50,000 capital stock required, there was a meeting electing the first board of directors with Schenck as president and Little as head of directors. Other officers were Asbury Fountain, Garrett P. Conover, Samuel Stillwell, and John A. Vanderbilt. Sixteen months after the charter was granted, the Farmers and Merchants Bank could begin to do banking business and proceeded to do so in the store building owned by Little on the site of what was once known as the Gelhaus or Commercial Block. Little was designated cashier. He had to take this on faith as no salary was stipulated for him. He did eventually receive $500 for his services in organizing the bank and being its cashier for the first year.

Little and Fountain were named a committee to get plates to print the notes that the bank would issue. It should be explained that the bank had to issue its own notes when someone borrowed money, to give the borrower means of payment that would have general acceptability. Among the images depicted on the bank script were historical figures, such as George Washington, Benjamin Franklin, or the Marquis de Lafayette, or mythical figures like Ceres, Vulcan, Mercury, and a

Several local businessmen owned the eighteenth-century home at 298 Main Street, including DeLafayette Schanck, his nephew Roelef V. Schanck, and Jacob R.V. Lefferts. DeLafayette Schanck was one of the founders of the Farmers and Merchants Bank and Lefferts was instrumental in the creation of Matawan's lakes. (Courtesy of Willett A. Rhodes.)

unicorn. Other images on the notes reflected the rural nature of the area, such as a farmer plowing, agricultural instruments, a blacksmith, and a drover with cattle. The bank was compelled by law to keep a reserve of gold and silver for redemption of its notes on demand.

At the June 1832 meeting, committees were appointed to get an iron keg in which to keep the bank's valuables and to look for a building in which to do business. The following month, the bank declared its first dividend, 4 percent for the prior six months. Four years later, a contract was taken with Mr. Simpson's lumberyard (which had been established the previous year) for the erection of a brick building at a cost of $3,400. The building served the bank until 1914 when a new building was erected next door. The new bank "was a model for construction of bank buildings in this area for the next 30 years." After World War II, the interior was changed to conform with modern bank design and the enclosed tellers' cages were done away with.

Among the interesting stories of the bank is that of the steamer *Monmouth*. In 1834, the bank granted credit to a group who wanted to purchase a steamboat. A few years later the group ran into difficulties, and by 1839 had only $2,500 to repay the $8,000 loan. The steamer *Monmouth* was sold at sheriff's sale; the bank bid on it and won. According to the bank's history, "the bank's loss was a negligible one" and the community had its steamer back.

There were many changes in the period 1800 to 1880 in the religious life of area residents with the formalization of several congregations and the great revivals of the Second Great Awakening. According to the history of the Presbyterian Church, "From that time (1777) until the present (1820), a period of above forty years, there has been no regular organized Church in this place," meaning that there was no regularly assigned minister, as supply ministers preached on a regular basis. In one attempt to obtain a minister, in 1816, a subscription list was created where church members would pledge to pay a certain amount toward the pastor's salary. Unfortunately, according to the history, no one signed the pledge. After being ordained in June 1798, Reverend George Spafford Woodhull served as pastor of congregations in Princeton and Cranbury before coming to Middletown Point as pastor of the Presbyterian congregation where he spent the last two years of his life until he died on December 25, 1834. Not all relationships between ministers and their congregation were amicable. Early in 1840, Reverend Joseph L. Shafer sued the congregation for owed salary and the old church building was sold at sheriff's sale. According to John Stillwell in *Historical and Genealogical Miscellany Data Relating to the Settlement and Settlers of New York and New Jersey*, the sale was insufficient to meet Shafer's claim, but Robert Little made up the $60 difference.

According to tradition, the last service at the Mt. Pleasant church was held in 1839. The congregation moved out after finding the church filled with smoke as a result of a defective chimney and green firewood. For the next two years, the congregation held services at Phillips Academy located at Church and Jackson Streets while the Presbyterian congregation acquired a lot on Main Street. The

The Presbyterian congregation has had to overcome several fires, including two that destroyed their sanctuaries. After the disastrous Christmas 1955 fire, this sanctuary was built on Route 34. Photographed at its 1958 raising, the steeple was a gift in memory of Spafford Schanck Jr., who died during World War II. (Courtesy of the First Presbyterian Church.)

cornerstone for the Main Street church building was laid during the summer of 1841 and the building dedicated the following year. The cost of the building was $3,010.66 and the noted American architect Stanford White designed the tower. A lecture hall was added in 1876 at a cost of $2,000. The Mt. Pleasant building was bought by Simon Arrowsmith and moved to his farm, now the site of Buttonwood Manor. It was used for storage at the dock site, then later as a barn.

Matawan had no Baptist church for more than 100 years after its founding. According to Reverend Lewis W. Kisenwether Jr. in *First Baptist in Matawan: A Constant Testimony*, Reverend Thomas Roberts, pastor from 1825 to 1837 of the Old First Baptist Church in Middletown, New Jersey, "began traveling on occasion to preach to those of Middletown Point," preaching in the homes of two local individuals, Mrs. Rachel Bent and John Disbrow. Later visiting ministers preached from time to time at the tavern in the village. When the First Baptist Church of Keyport was organized in 1840, its pastor began regular visits once a month to Middletown Point. Significant changes for the Baptist congregation came in December 1849, when a lot was purchased at 260 Main Street from Thomas I. Bedle at a cost of $200. Construction began on a meetinghouse, which was completed in October the following year with the Reverend Job Gaskill as the congregation's first pastor. It is interesting to note that according to the church

Matawan's Baptist congregation's first building did not contain a baptismal pool. Baptisms were held in the creek at a place called Gravelly Point, and were conducted in all seasons of the year. The sanctuary at 232 Main (center) was built with an indoor baptismal pool, but no steeple. A fiberglass steeple was added in 1970.

history, Gaskill wasn't paid a salary for the year he served the congregation as "both he and his wife had ample funds to see to their needs."

One of the first challenges the congregation faced was a familiar one of the time—fire. On Sunday, February 14, 1858, a fire destroyed the meetinghouse. It was reported in *The New Jersey Coast in Three Centuries* that not only was the loss total, but the insurance had lapsed. With no sanctuary, the congregation met in Washington Hall with supply pastors. Washington Hall was located in the Commercial Block at 192 Main Street at the location of the present Masonic lodge and was destroyed in the great fire of 1901. In late 1859, the congregation got a new minister, Reverend John E. Barnes, and the 77 members voted to sell the lot at 260 Main Street for not less than $300.

The property at 232 Main was purchased and a new building completed at a cost of $3,300. At the time the new building was dedicated in August 1860, James Buchanan, the 15th president of the United States, was in the White House facing the threats of southern states seceding from the Union. This new church was built without a steeple and did not have one until the summer of 1970, when a fiberglass steeple was installed. When a baptismal service was being held, the pulpit was shifted to another place and the flooring lid over the pool lifted. This arrangement prevailed until the early 1900s when the baptismal pool was moved to the left-hand corner of the sanctuary.

Early records of Methodist congregations in Monmouth County show there were few members in the county's early years. In 1779, there were only about 200

Methodists in the entire state of New Jersey. Methodists from the Middletown Point area went to Blue Ball, as Adelphia was then called, where the quarterly meetings were held. Circuit riders went from station to station on their assigned circuit, conducting preaching services. Due to their efforts, the numbers of believers grew and Methodist societies were formed. Sometime in 1826, prayer meetings and a Methodist class meeting began to be held at Middletown Point and the Society of Methodists at Middletown Point was formed. Through the efforts of the circuit rider preachers, the number of members in the Methodist society grew to 25 and gradually took on the form of a regular church. On July 11, 1835, the date future congregations were to use as the date of the founding of the church, a milestone was reached when the Society of Methodists at Middletown Point incorporated and took the name "The Trustees of the Methodist Episcopal Church." Although there were only 25 members enrolled at the time of incorporation, five of which were African Americans, the trustees went about building a church and dedicated it the following year. By this time, the number of Methodists in the state had grown from 200 in 1779 to 17,760 in 1837.

The first Methodist Church in town was described by Franklin Ellis in his 1885 history as being "back there among the horse barns" because it was built on what is now called Jackson Street behind the homes on Main Street. Purchased for the sum of $100, stipulated in lawful money of the United States, the lot

No longer "back among the horse barns," the Main Street sanctuary of the Methodist Episcopal Church was a prominent feature of Matawan's downtown. Photographed in front of Cherry Hall, the congregation's entry in the 1964 Tercentennial Parade, resembling the sanctuary, won the prize for "Most Impressive." (Courtesy of Matawan United Methodist Church at Aberdeen.)

could be traced back to Richard Frances in whose home early services were held. The cost of the church at 173 Jackson Street was about $1,800. Prayer meetings continued to be held in private homes and Joel Carhart's wheelwright shop for several years until Asbury Fountain Sr. built a lecture room adjoining the church. By 1841, the congregation had grown large enough so that it became independent of the Freehold Circuit and was appointed its own resident pastor, Reverend Zerrubbabel Gaskill.

The Jackson Street church continued to be used until 1855 when the congregation sold the building to Tunis Hubbard for $1,000 and moved into a new church building at the intersection of Main Street and Ravine Drive. Of Greek architecture, the 40-foot-by-70-foot red brick Methodist Episcopal Church was a major landmark in downtown Matawan with its steeple visible from most of the town and the church presenting a dramatic view as visitors came up Ravine Drive. The cornerstone was laid on June 13, 1854. Upon completion of the basement on November 5, 1854, a dedication service was held. At that time, it was decided not to finish the main audience room until it could be completed without debt. The following year, it was decided that the debt had been sufficiently reduced, and near the end of the summer of 1855, the building was completed at a total cost of about $11,000. Over the years, some of the changes to the church were more noticeable than others, such as the bell installed in the steeple in 1889 or the addition of a clock in the bell tower in 1914. In the 1880s, horse sheds were erected at the rear of property and used until they were eventually torn down almost 50 years later. Between 1907 and 1922, nine stained-glass windows were installed in the church.

There were other changes to come for the Matawan congregation. Over the years, they would parent three other congregations as members transferred to create churches in Jacksonville (later called Cheesequake), Cliffwood, and Morganville, and eventually move from the borough to the township. In 1843, a part of the African-American membership split off from the congregation and organized the African Methodist Episcopal Church.

According to the 1957 *History of Matawan Township*, the Cliffwood Community Methodist Church is the oldest church in Aberdeen Township, having been organized in the early 1840s. The following quote written by District Superintendent J.B. Haines from the 1908 *Minutes of the New Jersey Conference* tells much about the Cliffwood congregation: "The little church at Cliffwood is a loyal, heroic, faithful band of Christians, doing their work in the name and with the spirit of the Lord, showing special interest in the cause of foreign missions." On May 31, 1854, the trustees of the Cliffwood congregation purchased a lot for $75 from John Ivins and his wife Isabella, two members of the congregation. Later that year, a church was built on the lot. The money to build the church was obtained by subscription and church festivals, with much of the labor for the actual construction of the building being contributed. Those credited with being most influential in bringing about the establishment of the church were Thomas Porter, Jefferson Rogers, Steven Bogardus, Mrs. Thomas Porter, Henry Young,

David Hunter McAlpin, William Hughes, and Hendrick Van Cleaf. In 1899, the Cliffwood church building was struck by lightning and the structure so badly damaged that it had to be practically rebuilt. A parsonage was built in 1893 during the pastorate of J.B. Adams at a cost of $900.

The church sanctuary continued to be improved with new windows, pews, and an entrance. An adjoining Sunday school building was also added. W.P. Strickland reported in the 1895 *New Jersey Conference Minutes*, "New horse sheds have been erected at Cliffwood and paid for, and $100 has been paid on the debt of the parsonage. A new organ has also been paid for." The concept of member equity continued with the church even after the Methodist congregation was dissolved in 1981 due to declining membership. When the congregation of the Aberdeen Christian Center Church took over the structure later that year, much of the renovation and remodeling was done by the members. The Harvest Time Assembly of God is the most recent congregation to worship in the 1854 church building, the oldest in both Aberdeen and Matawan.

Trinity Episcopal Church was founded in 1850 through the liberality of Colonel John Travers, who resided at the mouth of the Cheesequake Creek. The cornerstone for the building at 74 Main Street was laid that spring, and the church was completed and consecrated in June the following year. The iron cross atop the belfry was a gift of friends in Keyport in 1859. In June 1851, the congregation consisted of 15 members. The first recorded collection at the church was $20.27, which was taken at the consecration service. The Reverend Fernando C. Putnam

This site marks the birthplace of the St. James AME Zion Church on Atlantic Avenue. Reverend James Simmons would become the congregation's first pastor.

was appointed missionary to the congregation and can be considered its first rector. Putnam resigned after two years, and the pulpit was serviced for many years by students from the General Theological Seminary and by a succession of ministers assigned by the archdeacon of the Diocese. Trinity became an assisted parish in 1926, and from then until 1958 was under the supervision of Saint Peter's in Freehold or Saint Mary's in Keyport.

Trinity Episcopal Church obtained full parish status in 1958. The congregation's first rectory on Wyckoff Street proved to be too small and a building was purchased at 142 Broad Street. Reverend Caroll B. Hall, a seminary student who was later ordained a priest, became the congregation's first full-time rector in 1961 and serviced the parish for 11 years. As a result of increased population in the late 1950s and early 1960s, the Main Street building with its seating capacity of only 75 no longer accommodated the growing congregation. In December 1966, the church acquired a 4-acre tract on Ryers Lane at West Court in the Freneau section of the borough. The Freneau building was dedicated in June 1968 and continues to be used as of the writing of this history. Unlike the old church on Main Street, the new building was a contemporary architectural style featuring laminated wood arches as the structural supports with an exterior of cedar shingles.

When William Little opened the Middletown Point Academy on Church and Jackson Streets in 1834, it had two students. Over the years, the building was used as the Middle District School and as a barn by James Conover. It was later moved to the end of Church Street and made into a double house (now numbers 1 and 3).

This three-story Italianate structure on Church Street, built in 1857, was the home of a locally prominent private school, the Glenwood Institute/Matawan Military Academy, for 58 years. This image shows the west end of the building (c. 1909). (Courtesy of the Madison Township Historical Society.)

A meeting in the front room of Matilda Conover's Atlantic Avenue home in 1843 marked the organization by Richard Little and his daughter Matilda of what would become St. James AME Zion Church. After subsequent meetings, the decision was made to erect a church. A site on Atlantic Avenue was deeded to the congregation in 1847 by James Jamison for $20. A church was built in 1851 and used for the next 46 years. In 1897, Reverend R.L. Butler purchased the lot at 100 Atlantic Avenue from Loun Little, brother of Matilda Conover, and the former Mt. Pleasant School was moved there for use as the congregation's church.

For much of the nineteenth century, not only local students but outsiders from as far away as Louisiana came to Middletown Point to get their education. William Little opened the Middletown Point Academy on the corner of Church and Jackson Streets in 1834. William Cooley was engaged to start the school, which was conducted in one room and had two pupils—the children of the sponsor. Eleven persons each agreed to put up $50 for construction of a 44-foot-by-26-foot schoolhouse, which was erected in 1838. Board could be obtained in good families for $2.25 per week. Tuition for the basic curriculum was $4. The school was co-ed; males could have languages and higher mathematics for $6, while females could take drawing, painting, fancy work, and embroidery for $6, or music for $10. Slightly over 20 years after its founding, academy stockholders subscribed $2,000 for a new building. The move across the street was accompanied by a name change, as the school became the Collegiate Institute of Middletown Point.

Brevet Colonel Charles Jefferson Wright was superintendent of the Matawan Military Academy and instructor of military science and tactics. He was a descendent of Samuel Wright, a famous fighter in the early days of the Massachusetts Colony. This image was taken from the Matawan Military Academy booklet (c. 1909). (Courtesy of Madison Township Historical Society.)

The school was later called the Glenwood Collegiate Institute and the Matawan Military Academy. Competition from free public high schools forced the academy to close in 1915.

Among the more notable students who attended the school was Garrett Augustus Hobart of Marlboro, who served as United States vice president from 1897 to 1899 under William McKinley, and New Jersey Governor Joseph D. Bedle. Although she had not yet made her mark as an author, Miriam Coles, later Miriam Coles Harris, also attended the institute. Her 1860 work *Rutledge* was described as the thrilling bestseller of the day. Perhaps the most distinguished teacher at the school was Robert Laird Borden, a young man of 19 who came to the institute from Nova Scotia in 1872 to teach mathematics and the classics. Borden would later become prime minister of Canada.

Philetus Phillips headed the school from 1836 to 1844, so for a time the school was known as the Phillips Academy. In addition to being headmaster, Phillips also was an inventor. He invented a chicken coop where the hens could open and close the door. He also came up with a siding where the outer covering resembled light-colored stone. In an experiment pre-dating stucco, Phillips used his new siding on a Jackson Street house.

Before the days of graded public schools, four district schools and private schools like the Glenwood Collegiate Institute were the main educational institutions in Matawan. The earliest record of education in Matawan goes back to 1755 with a mention of a school to be privately opened by Robert Savage. Public education in the 1800s was provided by district schools, the earliest of which appears to be Mt. Pleasant, in use in the 1830s. Curriculum of these schools did not extend much beyond the three R's—reading, 'riting, and 'rithmetic. The district school teachers often had beginning students to eighth grade under their charge. The opinion in an 1874 local editorial regarding a proposed state law to make school compulsory up to 14 years of age is interesting, as it shows a divergence from what is commonly accepted today. The commenter wrote in part, "this might do for Germany and other monarchs, but we cannot see how such a law can be compatible with our republican institutions." Before school became compulsory, there was no formal graduation in order to finish school—a student simply quit.

In 1895, it was decided to build a centralized building on Broad Street to replace the various district schools. The original building had eight rooms, was not of fireproof construction, and cost $16,000. By 1908, enrollment had increased so that an addition to the school was necessary. A separate high school was built next to the grammar school in 1923 to reduce overcrowding and offered four courses of study: normal, classical, scientific, and commercial. The Matawan school system remained basically the same until the 1960s when several additional schools were built. By 1972, to accommodate increased enrollment, the school system had seven elementary schools, two middle schools, and a high school.

Although no battles were fought in New Jersey, the Civil War (1861–1865) still had a major impact on the local residents. According to Francis A. Walker, head of the 1870 census, "For nearly four years an average body of a million and a half of men, from 18 to 45 years of age, were withdrawn from domestic life." During the

These are not soldiers at camp, but students at the Matawan Military Academy on their annual outing in 1909. (Courtesy of Madison Township Historical Society.)

Civil War, central New Jersey sent more than its required quotas into the Union Army. Individuals formed recruiting parties and toured their municipalities and adjacent countryside until the desired number for a company was secured. One description of how local men answered President Abraham Lincoln's August 1862 call for 300,000 men to serve nine months was described in an early September issue of the *Monmouth Democrat*:

> On Saturday noble men from the several townships came pouring in to swell the lists of volunteer patriots who are willing to live or die for their country's honor. They came with a will . . . They came in wagons and on foot; with fife and drum, and full brass band, pouring forth the strains of martial music; with banners waving in the breeze, they came, a host of freemen, to save their townships from the stigma of the draft, and help to preserve the existence of the Union. Matteawan, whose loyalty has been mistrusted, was among the earliest in, with more than her full number, bearing a banner with the words, "Mattawean—full quota."

Although some New Jersey units were comprised of residents from specific towns, others were made up of men from throughout the state. So not everyone from Middletown Point served in the same unit. In fact, there are even records

One of the early ministers to the Methodist congregation at Cliffwood was Reverend Joseph Garrison, who served the congregation from 1872 to 1873. At the outbreak of the Civil War, Garrison rode horseback from Illinois to Cape May County, New Jersey in order to join a New Jersey regiment. (Courtesy of Reverend Thomas White.)

of New Jersey men serving in out-of-state units. Of the 37 infantry regiments organized in New Jersey between 1861 and 1865, only the 29th New Jersey Volunteers could claim to be a virtually all-Monmouth unit. According to Stephens in *From Our Correspondent With the 29th Regiment*, "They made no desperate stands or gallant charges. They held no vital positions against insurmountable odds or performed acts of heroism that have entered into legend." Yet between September 1862 and June 1863, their story held the attention of local residents. In *To Monmouth From M.C.K. (With Love Yet)*, Melvin C. Krampf described the roster of Captain Vincent W. Mount's company, including several Middletown Point men: Isaac Van Dorn, William Forman, Nelson H. Hart, M. Hoease, and E.F. Disbrow. Another local man, William Henry Lloyd from Freneau, was a medical lieutenant at the Siege of Vicksburg.

A product of Lincoln's August 1862 call for volunteers, the companies of the 29th were organized by the various local municipalities of Monmouth and Ocean Counties. Company I was organized in Middletown Point by local men, together with the extra men from Company E and other companies. The ten companies of the 29th were assembled in early September 1862 at Camp Vredenburgh, located approximately 2 miles west of the Freehold business district. Journalist and militia officer Edwin F. Applegate was elected colonel. The 29th regiment left Camp Vredenburgh for war in late September 1862 with 39 officers and 909 enlisted men. It returned with 36 officers and 706 men.

The October 2, 1862 issue of the *Monmouth Democrat* described the sending off of the unit:

> On Sabbath afternoon the gallant 29th left Camp Vredenburgh for the seat of war. A large crowd was in attendance to see the boys off. Sad were the many farewells taken. Strong men wept like children, on bidding good-bye to wives. The scenes at camp, attending the bustle of departure, were in strange contrast with what should be the Sabbath observance.

The regiment was transferred in late November to the Army of the Potomac where they were assigned to the provost guard (military police). At the December 1862 Battle of Fredericksburg, Company I was one of several companies from the 29th that patrolled the streets of the town, while the battle raged on the outskirts. When the Army of the Potomac was withdrawn following their failure to defeat the Confederate Army commanded by Robert E. Lee, four companies of the 29th (including Company I) covered the retreat. The following January, the 29th was transferred to a combat unit, the Third Brigade, First Division, I Corps, and would stay with this unit until their discharge. The men suffered through the January 1863 "Mud March," an attempt to turn Lee's flank, which was defeated by torrential rains that turned the dirt roads of Virginia to a quagmire. As the Army of the Potomac marched northwards in June 1863 in pursuit of Lee in the campaign that would result in the Battle of Gettysburg, the 29th received orders to return home. The troops arrived home and were given a parade and a celebratory reception at the Freehold Fair Grounds. Their nine months of service came to an end in June 1863, when they were formally mustered out of the army.

During the regiment's service, local newspapers kept their readers, many of whom had friends and relatives in military service, informed of the unit's activities. As only the most prosperous city newspapers could afford to send correspondents to cover the war, small newspapers depended on local soldiers for first-hand news, printing letters that they received from the soldiers. Sergeant Benjamin Lawrence of Company H wrote home about his early days in the service as the unit traveled by rail to Washington, D.C.: "We reached Philadelphia about a quarter before eight that evening, when we formed in line and marched up to the ladies saloon." Dinner prepared by the kind ladies of the city was cold boiled ham, bread and butter, pickles, coffee, and cheese. As the troops marched in line the 1.25 miles back to the depot, "along the street it was a continual stream of shaking hands, and bidding good bye and the cries of 'God Bless You,' and grant you safe return."

Life in camp was described as follows: drill about two hours a day with the muskets and have dress parade every afternoon at 5 p.m. Other correspondence described food and shelter in camp—and an added surprise:

> We layed on the ground all that night, exposed to the night air. We were all tired and slept as good as if we had slept on feather beds. The cows came inside of our lines the next morning, and the boys took their tin cups and canteens and filled them with milk, and we had hard bread and milk for breakfast.

Another correspondent described a different aspect of military life:

> At a meeting of the officers held on Wednesday night, it was proposed to take up a collection for the purpose of buying stoves for the Hospital tents and boards to floor the same, for the comfort of the sick, none being allowed by the Government in the field service. The requisite amount was subscribed and paid on the spot.

Local Middletown Point men in the 29th included the assistant surgeon Dr. Judson C. Shackleton and Jacob R. Schenck, regimental quartermaster. Schenck earned promotions to sergeant, then second lieutenant. Among letters published in local papers by Schenck under the pen "Casual" was the following excerpt:

> I am sorry to inform your readers that sickness has reduced our ranks very much since our departure from Tennallytown. We are now under marching orders, expecting to leave every hour, and our surgeons were ordered to report to the Brigade Surgeon all not able to undergo "a march." Surprising as it may appear, this day we have reported for duty in the 29th a little rising six hundred men, it is six hundred and fourteen.

Soldiers marched down Main Street, between Little Street and Ravine Drive, in front of Mahoney's grocery. The carriage factory on the corner of Ravine Drive and Main Street can be seen behind the end of the troop.

> We have absent, sick, and otherwise, two hundred and eight-six, making an aggregate (present and absent) of nine hundred men. Our aggregate when mustered at Camp Vredenburgh was nine hundred and fourty-two, making a loss of forty-two by death, discharges, and desertions.

Although he did not serve with the Middletown Point company, Charles Wardell did serve with the 29th and became a longtime Matawan resident after the war. The following journal entries describe his days: Friday, September 12, 1862: "heavy rain. Had a drill before breakfast. Received for company today 45 loaves bread, 144 pounds bacon. Attended prayer meeting in barracks this evening." Wednesday, November 1862: "rainy muddy and disagreeable. W.S. Worthley received a box from Eatontown. I got a pair mittens, some stationary, 2 lemons, some candy and cake. Most of the contents of the box were spoiled. The box has been at Adams office in Washington since Nov. 1." Although it was wartime, some troops were able to celebrate Christmas, according to a December 25, 1862 entry: "had stew for dinner made of pork, onions, and potatoes. Hung up my stocking but Santa Claus did not fill it. Drew a gallon of rye whiskey from the quartermaster and distributed it among the boys."

Not everyone in the area wholeheartedly supported the Northern policies. While many local men were serving in the Union Army, the famous "Peace Meeting" was held in Middletown on August 29, 1862. The petition calling for the peace meeting was signed by 168 prominent Monmouth County citizens.

Myron Diggin took this photo of a man named "Tom," who lived in the Matawan area and was born a slave.

Many of the instigators of the rally, which was looked upon as traitorous by the war-stirred patriots, had been slaveholders prior to the abolition of slavery in New Jersey in the early 1840s. According to Mandeville in his history of Middletown, "The real purpose (of the meeting) was to express the sentiments of a large number of people who thought the conduct of the Civil War a failure and who thought the states wherein secession existed should be allowed to secede in peace."

Five thousand armed men assembled in Middletown, intent upon breaking up the meeting. Among the signers of the peace petition was Joseph C. Arrowsmith of Middletown Point. As he rode home to Matawan on horseback, Mrs. Thomas B. Stout, a strong Republican and Unionist, stood at her gate and remarked, "Joseph, how did you make out?" and his reply as recorded was, "Whipped, by God, Aunt Amelia." In the March 1863 Matawan Township election, one voter expressed his sentiments by writing in "Jefferson Davis" for tax collector.

Slavery existed in Monmouth County from the earliest days of white settlement in the 1660s. One prevalent use of slavery was on a small farm. Most Monmouth County farms were well under 300 acres with many of 100 or less. The probate records of the first generation of slave owners in Monmouth County reveal small-scale farming with slaves often the most important possession. According to Graham R. Dodge in *African Americans in Monmouth County During the Age of the American Revolution,* by 1770, about 40 of Monmouth County African Americans were free, or about 4.5 percent of the black population of 900. Although an act was passed in 1820 by the New Jersey Legislature for the emancipation of the slaves, they were not all set free at once. A system of gradual emancipation was adopted by which the young people obtained their freedom when they came of age, while the masters were obliged to take care of the older African Americans as long as they lived. According to Leonora McKay in *The Blacks of Monmouth County*, in 1840, there were still 674 slaves in New Jersey.

Early residents of Matawan were not all white. At one point in time in the town's history, the area across Lake Matawan centered on Atlantic Avenue was known as Africa. Early records of the Matawan Methodist Episcopal Church listed the race of the members. The 1837 Sabbath School listed six African Americans on its rolls, among them Jane Willet. Her obituary in the April 2, 1881 edition of the *The Matawan Journal* provides evidence that the Matawan area was familiar with slavery:

> The Last Relic of Slavery in Matawan—Died in this village, at the homestead of Samuel Stillwell, deceased, now the residence of A.H. Harris, Esq. On Monday last, March 18, 1881, Jane Willet, aged 79 year and 10 months. The above aged colored woman, familiarly known as "Aunt Ginny," had been in the same family in which she died for nearly sixty-six years, and has lived to see four generations of Stillwells and their descendants.
>
> She was purchased as a slave, while that institution existed in New Jersey, in 1815, by Samuel Stillwell, from Joseph Holmes, grandfather of Mr. Chrineyonce Holmes. Her age was such that when the law was passed in this state for the manumission of all slaves under a certain age, it did not reach her case. She was, however, given her choice, and preferred to remain with the family, and had lived with them up to her death.

The July 1809 issue of *The American*, published in Trenton, New Jersey, advertised for sale a 24-year-old African-American woman named Lydia and her daughter. At the time, Lydia was a convict in the state prison whose term was nearly expired. The advertisement also noted that Lydia had formerly belonged to Mr. John O'Briant of Middletown Point.

In 1917, in his "Jersey Genealogy" column of the *Newark Evening News*, historian William S. Hornor wrote, "the honor of longest family lineage went to negroes." Cudjo Minkerson, who died in 1814, possessed parts of two lots that were the original Mt. Pleasant settlement. Tradition has it that not far from the beginning of the eighteenth century, an African of pure blood married a Mohingson woman. The child was originally called Cudjo Mohingson, which was later corrupted to Minkerson. Hornor also wrote that Cudjo was probably the first instance of an African American owning land in New Jersey.

5. ERA OF INDUSTRY AND RESORT

The technological advances and industrial development of the first seven decades of the nineteenth century continued in the last three decades of the century, fueled partly by the discovery of oil at Titusville, Pennsylvania. As a state, New Jersey continued its earlier emphasis on developing industry. The 1915 *Industrial Directory of New Jersey* reported a 25.3 percent increase in the number of persons engaged in the manufacturing industry between 1905 and 1914, even though 40 percent of the industries still used horsepower. A shift in population was also reported in the directory. In 1890, approximately 60 percent of the state's residents lived in an urban setting. That number had increased to almost 79 percent by 1915. Between 1900 and 1910, the state's population increased by 34.7 percent, the largest increase for all states east of the Rockies except for Florida. In 1860, New Jersey was the 21st most populated state in the nation and, by 1915, had moved up to 9th place.

Strangers passing through twenty-first-century Matawan would have little idea of the amount of manufacturing that went on there in the past. Matawan became an early home of manufacturing industries and continued to be so in the late 1800s. Although the industries started during this time are no longer in existence, for many years they not only supplied products to the region and the nation, but also provided employment for hundreds of local residents. Barrels, crates, ceramic floor and wall tile, matches, piano plates, and pianos were all once manufactured locally. In the late 1800s, the Colonial Match factory in Matawan was sold to the Diamond Match Company of New York for $50,000. The principal industries in operation in Cliffwood listed in the 1915 Industrial Directory were the Cliffwood Brick Company, employing 600 persons; Lenox Brick Company; and the Oschwald Brick Company, employing 100 persons.

Although considered an unusual product today, horse manure was another local product that was used as a heating fuel. Between 1901 and 1907, Bernard Campbell and Company gathered and shipped horse manure. The letterhead showed Judson Conover in Matawan, who was most likely their local representative; an office in New York City at Eighth Avenue and 34th Street; and dumps at the foot of 25th Street in Brooklyn. The firm stated that they delivered their product from stable to farm, and that they gathered and sold by rail and water 100,000 tons per

Among the dangers of the brick industry were being killed when a kiln collapsed, being caught in equipment, or being injured by a runaway horse or mule teams. This image shows Farry's Brick Yard, c. 1902. The kilns were on the NY & LB rail line between the Matawan and Hazlet stations. (Courtesy of New Jersey Geological Survey.)

year. In addition to horse manure, a 1922 piece of Conover letterhead listed him as manufacturer of Conover Oyster Shell Lime and the maker of the Original Lakewood Tomato Crate.

Although a fairly small concern with only 20 employees, Monmouth Woodworking Company was another crate manufacturer that was supposed to have started making crates in 1919. Two other firms also produced crates. Established in 1906, the Frank Anderson Basket Factory on Atlantic Avenue made peach and apple baskets, and tomato and berry crates (principally for the home market in Monmouth County). A 1918 letterhead for the firm also advertised all kinds of telephone poles among the lumber the firm sold in the hardware division. At one time, the firm manufactured an average of 150,000 to 200,000 baskets a year. The factory burned down in the spring of 1940. In 1927, Henry

Geran erected a one-story wooden structure, 100 feet by 80 feet, on Sutphin Avenue near the railroad tracks in Freneau for the purpose of making crates and boxes. He operated the factory until 1931 when he retired and the business was taken over by Herbert Burlew, who eventually went into partnership with Elwood MacElvaine of Englishtown. The Burlew and MacElvaine factory manufactured crates for tomatoes, raspberries, strawberries, and apples using North Carolina pine. An advertisement in *The Matawan Journal* 1936 anniversary edition reported that the average time required to make a crate was two minutes.

Among the other products made in Matawan were pianos and piano plates. In 1900, Matawan Steel and Iron Company, Church Street, was started by Sidney B. Eggleston and Harry Bolte. Within seven years, they had $65,144.46 in assets and employed 100 persons. At the firm's tenth anniversary, the plant capacity was 200 piano plates a day; however, piano plates were not the firm's only product. A few years later, the firm advertised in the local press for other foundry work, such as manhole covers and castings to order. Wickham Company of New Jersey, a branch of a Springfield, Ohio company, bought out the firm and operated it for several years. One of the notable aspects of the company was the 1919 fire,

The original 50-foot by 200-foot building, erected in 1887 on Church Street by the Matawan Improvement Company for the Standard Shade Company, became a sophisticated industrial complex. It was later occupied by the Munning Loeb Company and Hanson–Van Winkle–Munning. This is the letterhead of the Antisell Piano Company, c. 1893.

described as the most destructive fire ever in town. Caused by an explosion of varnish, the fire destroyed 6,000 plates and 2 buildings of the factory, causing an estimated $100,000 in damage.

Fire was responsible for many business losses. The four-story brick and heavy pine timber building housing the Wason piano factory was totally destroyed by a June 1916 fire that started with an explosion on the first floor. At the time, the building was partially leased to the Synthetic Chemical Company, which manufactured phenol, asperin, salcyclic acid, and carbolic acid. Although the neighboring passenger station and Kennedy's hotel were saved, there was an estimated loss of $50,000 to the piano factory, including the destruction of 60 to 70 pianos in various stages of construction. Firemen initially fought the flames from the top of several empty boxcars on the tracks in front of the building. The fire also affected commuters as train service was shut down in both directions until after 10:30 p.m. because several lines of hose extended across the tracks.

Hanson–Van Winkle–Munning was another major firm in the area for many years that is no longer on the business landscape. The firm was started in 1911 as the Munning Loeb Company with 75 employees to make electroplating and buffing apparatus and supplies for all industries. By 1928, the firm had been renamed to Hanson–Van Winkle–Munning Company and had 400 employees. Between 1919 and 1948, other buildings were added on the site to the original 50-foot-by-200-foot building built in 1887 by the Matawan Improvement Company for the Standard Shade Company. Just before World War II, it covered 150,000 square feet and there were 300 people working there. During World War II, the firm made significant contributions to the war effort. A modern laboratory building was added to the complex in 1949.

Tile making in Monmouth County was centered in the neighboring towns of Matawan and Keyport. The major tile manufacturers in Matawan were Matawan Tile Company and the Atlantic Tile Manufacturing Company. In 1902, Bennet Eskesen, his brother, and Karl Mathiasen established the Matawan Tile Company to make floor and wall tile. A major fire occurred at the Matawan Tile Company plant in January 1916 that destroyed the main manufacturing building and its contents, a one-story machine shop, and a kiln. Although the firm survived the 1930s, while many other businesses did not, the looming cloud of World War II cemented the plant's closure.

In addition to architectural tile, a division of the company called the Progressive Art Tile Company made a variety of decorative items. The work of this division can easily be identified by its octagonal shape. One of the ceramic engineers at the firm was Harry Kahn. In the late 1920s, Kahn opened a decorator studio in his home. He later expanded and did business as the Tile Products Company, selling Harikan Art Products until entering military service in World War II. Some of the designs used on the firm's products were created by Hannah, Kahn's wife, who was also a decorator.

Less than a mile away from Matawan Tile on the east-west railroad tracks, another tile company, the Atlantic Tile Manufacturing Company, was started in

Co-founders Charles E. Barker (right) and Herbert Gittens are taking a break at the Atlantic Tile Manufacturing Company. At one time, 200 people worked a full-time daily schedule. Closed during the Depression, the plant reopened afterward with a reduced workforce of 80 employees.

1910 by Charles Barker, his father Edward, and Herbert Gittens. Originally, the firm was a small operation with only one kiln in which unglazed floor tile was made. In 1919, the Atlantic Tile Manufacturing Company was sold to the Mosaic Tile Company of Zanesville, Ohio. With the resources of Mosaic behind it, the plant was greatly expanded to 90,000 square feet and additional buildings were erected to speed production. The Matawan plant ceased operations in 1964 with the closure of the parent company. In the late 1990s, the buildings were razed and a townhouse complex, the Crossing at Aberdeen, was built on the site.

Many changes came to the Matawans between 1870 and 1920, including the trolley, telephone, and development of Cliffwood Beach. Reverend Frank A. Slater began a landmark ministry at the First Baptist congregation on October 1, 1866. Slater would serve for 22 years, 3 months, and 17 days, a record of longevity in pastoral ministry that was not eclipsed until over 100 years later. Among the landmarks of his ministry, besides the length of time, was that he received the most members. Just three years after his arrival, the congregation was to experience a tremendous year of growth as 60 members joined the congregation. In 1901, the congregation purchased the house next to the church for $2,000 as a parsonage, which was used by nine pastors and their families until 1969 when it was replaced by a property in the Strathmore section of the township.

The Second Baptist Church was organized in 1889 as Berean Baptist Church when the founding members met in area homes. In spring 1890, they rented a room in Bissel Hall then situated on Spring Street. The following year, they acquired an abandoned skating rink on the corner of Jackson Street and Fountain Avenue and remodeled it for church use. The congregation used it until 1908, when it was destroyed by fire. A cornerstone was laid on June 22, 1913 and a one-story church building was erected on Orchard Street at a cost of $1,800 for the church and furnishings. In the summer of 1916, a mortgage burning was held and the building was enlarged the following year.

The late 1800s were the grand old days of the trolley. Intended to be a horse car line from Matawan to Keyport, the Keyport and Matawan Street Railway was incorporated in the spring of 1867. However, it took 20 years before the local papers were able to print the details of a possible line to be constructed by a group of Boston capitalists. One month after the notice, stone and rail were delivered to Keyport to enable the start of construction over the right-of-way of the old Keyport Plank Road. By 1890, there were 18 horse car companies in New Jersey with 230 miles of track, about 700 cars, and over 4,000 horses and mules. But electrification was coming and the horse-drawn vehicles would be made obsolete. Shortly after the dawning of the twentieth century, the trolley system was electrified and with electrification came the name of the Jersey Central Traction Company.

Although the original line from Matawan to Keyport had been extended to Freneau, plans to continue to Freehold were stopped when the Central Jersey Railroad refused the trolley permission to cross its tracks. That was not the only interaction between the trolley and the railroad—the trolley could not cross the railroad in Matawan. Riders could only take the trolley to the Matawan station. There they had to disembark, walk across the railroad tracks, and pick up the

From the late 1800s to 1923, local residents could ride the trolley. Although it ran from Freneau to Keyport, passengers had to get out and walk across the tracks to pick up a car on the other side, as the the trolley car could not cross the railroad tracks at the Matawan station. This image shows Main Street in 1910.

trolley on the other side either into Matawan and Freneau or over to Keyport, depending on which side of the tracks they started. According to *The Matawan Journal*, the trolley received a 1¢ fare increase in late 1918, raising the fare to 7¢. World War I hastened the trolley line's decline due to a shortage of replacement parts. The influence of the automobile began to be felt in the early 1920s. Between 1918 and 1923, more than 500 miles of trolley lines were abandoned in the state, of which the Jersey Central Traction Company contributed 36 miles. In July 1923, the trolley line received permission to halt operations and all services in the Bayshore area ended shortly thereafter.

One indication of progress was when the Bell Telephone Company started telephone service in the town. Even before the telephone, Matawan had a telegraph station. The telegraph line was installed in 1870. According to Rennselear Cartan, the railroad station was a telegraph office and so was his family's store, Cartan and Company at 90 Main Street. A tobacco tin was used to change the sound of the railroad telegraph and avoid confusion. In his *Notes on the Early History of Matawan, N.J. and Vicinity*, Cartan wrote about practicing on the telegraph key at night when there was little or no wire traffic. Unfortunately, one night he left the key open and it killed the entire line for two days between New York City and Bay Head.

Truancy would not be a problem when John Whitlock, truant officer, was on duty in his "modern" car. Cars replaced trolleys as the preferred mode of travel, beginning in the 1920s.

Although local residents were introduced to a telephone as early as 1878, it was not until about 1890 that regular service was provided when a switchboard was installed in the Aberdeen Inn near the train station. The first two telephones, both public, were installed at Slater's Drug Store and at the Aberdeen Inn. The first exchange in this section of the county was described as resembling an old-fashioned grandfather clock. Instead of the automatic switches of the later twentieth century, the heart of the early telephone system was a three-position switchboard located in a brick building on Main Street just below the railroad. Service in those days wasn't the click-click of the pre-touchtone dial phones. The caller would turn the crank in a box on the wall to contact the operator, who would then ring the number requested. According to Genevieve Donnell, one of the early operators, they were called the "hello" girls and their motto was "voice with the smile." Her initial starting pay was $3. When she retired in 1920, Donnell was making $36 per week. As more telephone lines were needed, the exchange outgrew the Aberdeen Inn and a larger exchange was installed in the Close building at 21 Main Street. In 1916, service was transferred from the old magneto central office to more modern equipment in the Walling building in Keyport. Turning a crank to get an operator was no longer necessary. All local residents had to do was to pick up the phone to make the connection.

At the turn of the twentieth century, social and civic clubs were popular. Some had names like the Arlington Club, Pastime Social Club, Patriotic Order Sons of America, and the Magnolia Club. The Matawan and Freneau Euchre Club, which was organized in the fall of 1912, was disbanded in late 1936, supposedly due to "the growing enthusiasm for bridge." Dominos were a popular pastime for a while. Established in 1896, the Domino Club had weekly dues of 10¢ and met Friday evenings in members' homes. The Scientific Four Domino Club, whose members were William G. Bedle, Harry Walling, Elwood VanBrakle, and F. Howard Lloyd, was described in the local paper as "locally renowned." The paper also reported that the club was responsible for "one of the most complete and unique scoring methods for dominos ever known." According to the Bureau of Industrial Statistics of New Jersey, in 1915, fraternal orders were represented in the Matawans by lodges of Masons, Odd Fellows, Royal Arcanum, American Mechanics, Patrons of Husbandry, and the Red Men, most of which no longer have local chapters in the Matawan-Aberdeen area.

Although there were only six women at the first meeting when the Women's Club of Matawan was formed in 1915, 60 women were present at the third one. For many years, the club met in various homes and offices, and rented space from other organizations. The club's permanent headquarters at 199 Jackson Street was not purchased until 1962 when it acquired the former Sunday school building of the First Presbyterian Church for $10,000. The club had several significant firsts. The first club president, Mrs. Daniel E. Van Wickle, was the first woman in town to serve on the Board of Education and the second woman in the state to hold the position. Professional and working women are nothing new to the organization whose rosters over the years have included 14 lawyers, 9 doctors, 4 ministers, 53 teachers, and several nurses. The club's founder, Mrs. Beatrice Stern, was a lawyer in Newark, New Jersey.

Girl scouting began in Matawan when ten girls met at the home of Mrs. F.T. Taylor in early 1928 and a troop was formed under the sponsorship of the Matawan Women's Club. Five years later, a brownie troop was formed with 15 charter members. By the fall of 1940, Matawan had four troops. In 1969, there were a total of 896 girls registered in 33 troops meeting in the Matawan neighborhood, including sixteen brownie troops, twelve junior troops (seven in Strathmore and five in the borough), four cadet troops, and one senior troop.

Not all activities centered around small groups; some were town-wide events. Matawan's earliest strawberry festival was held in June 1878 at Washington Hall (192 Main Street, now the Masonic Lodge). According to the local paper, the following was provided to add interest:

> Mr. Stoll has made arrangements for a connecting wire from the telegraph line into the Hall to which will be attached the Speaking Telephone. This wire will be continuous with one running into Park Hall, Asbury Park, where a similar festival will be held, and those here will have the privilege of talking to their Matawan friends there, so many of whom reside in Asbury Park and Ocean Grove. Ten cents is almost no price for admission to such a treat.

In the early 1900s, a band of Romanian gypsies camped for several weeks each year in a thick group of trees in the Oak Shades section of the township, near St. Joseph's Church. Genevieve Donnell describes the arrival of the gypsy caravan in *Matawan Memories*: "The horses, resplendent with gay trappings and tinkling bells, pulled the covered wagons, and dark-haired children peeped out shyly from the canvas-covered vehicles." She described how the long full skirts of the women brushed the dusty road as they walked beside the horses and how their "beads and bangles harmonized with the brass bells on the harness of the horses." Many years later, the gypsy troop's yearly visits were still remembered by local residents.

There were other aspects to life in the township and the borough. The ten presidential tickets in 1900 offered a variety of platforms. The Silver Republicans offered William J. Bryan of Nebraska for president and Adlai E. Stevenson III for vice president on the platform that "There being no longer any necessity for collecting war taxes levied to carry on the war with Spain." The party also favored the immediate admission into the Union of the territories of Arizona, New Mexico, and Oklahoma. The 1901 election returns showed that Matawan Borough had 229 Republicans, 132 Democrats, and 5 votes for the prohibition line. Matawan Township had 143 Republicans, 179 Democrats, and 7 prohibition votes.

What has been described as the most disastrous fire in Matawan's history occurred in late January 1901. A series of fires engulfed the major part of the business district, causing losses of over $100,000. The fire enveloped the harness store and the bakery, then spread down the street until being stopped at the

One of the worst disasters in Matawan's history was the 1901 fire that destroyed several buildings in this section of Main Street, shown here in 1905. What is now the Masonic Lodge in the center was one of those that survived.

Knickerbocker Lodge (192 Main Street). The wind then changed direction, sending the fire northward up the street, where the brick opera house with Frank H. Slater's drugstore and Mahoney's grocery also caught fire. There was a claim of a firebug at work as two other unrelated fires were also discovered.

The 1901 fire was not the first major fire in the town. Less than ten years earlier, fire destroyed a home, several businesses, and damaged the Methodist Episcopal Church, Shock's tobacco store, and several small buildings. Supposedly, the flames started in Henry S. Terhune's law office by the upsetting of the office stove. The fires did not stop business development in town, as the Matawan Bank became the second bank in town in 1915.

The original township hall, a small wooden building at 93 Atlantic Avenue, was built in 1905. In 1957, a one-story brick building on Lower Main Street at Suydam Place was built to serve as the township municipal hall until after the

From 1892 to 1905, when this wooden, one-room building was erected at 93 Atlantic Avenue, township meetings were held in the Borough Hall. The township paid annual rent to the borough, which in turn rented the space from a private owner. Prior to this, the township used the Hook and Ladder Company No. 1, Washington Engine No. 1, and earlier still, John H. Farry's hotel. This picture was taken in 1957.

major development of the 1960s when a new township hall was built on Church Street in 1979.

Township assessor Charles A. Neidlinger reported in early 1916 that the death rate was 5 percent less than the average for the previous four years, or a ratio of 12 people out of 1,000. He was quoted in the local paper as saying, "This is, indeed, a low death rate and one that but few municipalities in the state can beat." The report continued that there is not a single case of infantile paralysis (polio) in the township, but Tucker Walling, age 14, was reported to health inspector George F. Keller as being sick with scarlet fever. The house and inmates were immediately placed under quarantine and an officer put on guard to see that the quarantine was enforced.

What might be the Matawans' claim to fame was a 1916 shark attack when Matawan was catapulted into the national limelight. The first attack in the area occurred in early July off Beach Haven, New Jersey, followed by another in Spring Lake a few days later. According to Dr. Richard Fernicola in *Twelve Days of Terror*, Charles E. Vansant's death "received minimal coverage by the northern New Jersey and New York newspapers," thus leaving the town unprepared for what was to come. For most of the week, the temperature hovered in the mid-80s, but on Wednesday, July 12, it spiked to 96 degrees. Young Lester Stillwell had completed 150 peach baskets by 1:45 p.m. and was dismissed early to go join his friends at the creek because of the heat. Although Vansant had been attacked several days earlier, the initial call to Chief John Mulsoff, town barber and chief of police, about a shark was dismissed because the townspeople simply could not believe that a shark could have made its way up a meandering tidal creek 16 miles from the open ocean. However, that disbelief disappeared after several boys, who had been swimming with Stillwell and had seen the dorsal and tail fin of a shark, ran into town calling out the alarm. In their panic and haste after seeing Stillwell disappear beneath the surface of the creek, the boys, who had been skinny-dipping, had forgotten to put their clothes back on.

Although 12-year-old Stillwell was the first local casualty, Stanley Watson Fisher, a 24-year-old dry cleaner, is the name more familiar to local residents. When Fisher and Red Burlew dove into the water to recover Stillwell's body, Fisher himself was attacked by the shark. After the local doctor, Dr. George C. Reynolds, devised a tourniquet using a piece of rope, Fisher was carried on a makeshift stretcher to the train station where he lay until just after 5 p.m., then was placed on a train for transport to Long Branch and Monmouth Memorial Hospital. While the train bearing Fisher made it to Long Branch in record time, Fisher died one hour after admission.

Fisher and Stillwell were not the only local people attacked. Joseph Dunn, age 12, and his 14-year-old brother Michael had traveled by train from New York City to Cliffwood to spend the day with their aunt. The boys met Jerry Hourihan, a friend who lived in Matawan, and went swimming at the brickyard dock in Matawan Creek to escape the heat, unaware of what had happened approximately a half mile away. The three boys heard a called warning of "shark" and began to leave the water. While Hourihan and Michael made it to shore, the shark caught Joseph and started to pull him away. Jerry and Michael formed a human chain to

Area creeks were not only sources of transportation, but were used for leisure activity as well. Although there have been several drownings in area lakes since they were created, the most famous water-related event was the 1916 shark attack.

rescue Joseph, and with the help of the brickyard superintendent Robert Thress, everyone made it to shore. Captain Thomas Cottrell, who arrived about that time, transported the two Dunn boys to the Wyckoff dock where he hoped Joseph would receive speedy care from the crew assembled for Fisher. Since Dunn's injuries and blood loss were less severe than Fisher's, he was transported by car to St. Peters Hospital in New Brunswick where he was treated and eventually released, surviving his encounter with the denizen of the deep.

Unlike the earlier attacks, the deaths of Fisher and Stillwell made the front page of papers all around the country as the news was spread rapidly along the telephone lines and the rail system. By nightfall, there were no fewer than 15 nets lining Matawan Creek. Loud blasts and gunshots could also be heard as local residents hoped to destroy the intruding shark with dynamite and rifles. Continuing the unusual saga, Fisher had accepted a $10,000 life insurance policy from Ralph Gorsline, an agent for London and Lancashire Indemnity, in exchange for the sale of a suit. After Fisher's death, since he was a singer in the Methodist Church choir, the family decided to purchase, in his memory, a stained-glass window for the front of the church. The inscription on the window said "In Loving Memory of Stanley W. Fisher" and a quote from the Gospel of John 15:13: "Greater love hath no man than this, that a man lay down his life for a friend."

Sharks are not the only sea creatures to have visited the Matawan-Aberdeen area over the years. In the summer of 1974, a 300-pound, 7-foot-long bottlenose

Swimming in the creeks was not the only way local residents could escape the summer heat, as both the water at Cliffwood Beach and the shady groves of Cliffwood provided alternate means of cooling off. This group (probably German immigrants) was just one of many who gathered at the groves in Cliffwood. (Behr Collection, 1909, Courtesy of the Aberdeen Township Historical Commission.)

Although the congregation no longer has the Fisher window, physical ties remaining between the Methodist sanctuary on Atlantic Avenue and its predecessor on Main Street include the Bennem Bell (front) and several paintings. The chancel rail from the Main Street church was used in the upstairs chapel of the new sanctuary.

dolphin visited Matawan Creek, unaware of the attention it attracted from as far away as Atlantic City. Eleven years later, an approximately 12-foot-long, 700-pound pilot whale washed ashore and was stranded on a township beach.

One of the major issues of the town in 1917 was the controversy surrounding the bell in the Methodist Episcopal Church steeple when John Terhune, who resided next to the church, filed a petition to stop its ringing. The 2,050-pound bell had been installed in the steeple in 1889 as a tribute to Catherine J. Bennem Brown from her husband Edward I. Brown. The problem arose when the bell, which had regularly been rung for church services, was connected to a clock so that it would strike the hours. The local residents themselves were divided over the clock. Some considered it a personal annoyance; others felt that the striking of the hours was a useful public service. The final decree, issued March 13, 1917 by his Honor Edwaren Walker, chancellor of the state of New Jersey, ordered that the bell not ring the hours, either day or night. According to the church history, after what was referred to as the "town clock" was silenced, two local men connected the clock mechanism to an automobile horn that sounded the hours for several days, until it too was silenced.

Before Matawan got modern firefighting equipment, several of the town's congregations were integral parts of the borough's defense against fire. A cistern was placed on the Methodist Episcopal Church grounds in 1879 for use in fighting fires in that part of town. For a period of time before the town's siren system was installed, because of its downtown location, the church's bell was used to alert the volunteer firemen to respond to fires. A rope hung down the outside of the building so the bell could be rung as the fire signal without having to enter the church. However, the practice had to be discontinued because of false alarms when mischievous youths rang the bell when there were no fires. At one time, the Presbyterian Church bell was also used as the fire alarm. The practice was discontinued when a more modern fire siren was installed on the roof of the borough hall.

During the first quarter of the twentieth century, local men again went to battle, as the United States declared war on Germany in the spring of 1917. One description wrote about "the sight of troops leaning out of trains and waving, the Liberty Loan rallies, the initial enthusiasm for war, and the subsequent ennui—men who left for camp and Europe and never came back—some buried there and others brought back to rest here." As during the Civil War, the enlistees were given large sendoffs. One local paper gave the following account of a 1917 sendoff for 47 men, including 26 men from Matawan-Keyport who left on Saturday, September 22 on the 8:21 a.m. train from the Matawan station. According to the account, there were 1,000 or more people at the station awaiting the men's arrival from Keyport where they had reported for roll call. Before departing to the station, Keyport Mayor O.O. Bogardus gave a speech, the Keyport Silver Band played, and Reverend T.B. Reynolds, pastor of the Reformed Church, offered a prayer for the men's protection and safety.

Besides the 75 automobiles that made the run to the Matawan station, the trolley company ran two extra cars. Two small cannons were fired as the men were boarding the train. As the train pulled from the station, all the factories in town blew their whistles in salute. Over the course of the next five years, more than 150 men from the borough and the township went into the service. Other men didn't go overseas, but served in the First Squadron Cavalry National Guard. The loss of manpower to military service was not the only effect on the local residents during World War I. Much local effort went into raising funds to support the war effort and the progress was reported in the local paper. For one drive, the United War Drive, the borough and township's combined quota was $3,500. The local paper proudly reported that $4,663 was raised. The May 16, 1919 *Matawan Journal* had a headline proudly exclaiming, "Matawan Exceeds Its Quota of $251,000 in Victory Loan Drive."

Not all the men who went "over there" returned. The doughboy statue in Matawan's Memorial Park has stars for the men who went to war and gave the ultimate sacrifice, including George Bublin, Charles S. Dexter, John James Furey, James Carney, and John Hourihan. Over the years, there have been other memorials to local fallen men. The Royal Order of Hibernians donated a stained-glass window in Furey's memory to St. Joseph's Roman Catholic Church in Keyport. A stained-glass window in the Methodist Episcopal Church on Main Street in the borough was dedicated in February 1919 to the boys who served in the army and navy during World War I.

The largest memorial to local servicemen is Memorial Park at the intersection of Broad and Main Streets. Established in 1922 with 37 charter members of

Dedicated on Armistice Day, November 11, 1927, "The Spirit of the American Doughboy" by famous sculptor E.M. Viquesney was placed in Memorial Park by members of the Matawan American Legion Auxiliary. This image shows the World War II plaque dedication ceremony on Memorial Day, 1965, in Memorial Park on Main Street.

former servicemen's wives and sisters, the American Legion Auxiliary raised over $200 by the sale of poppies and holding cake sales, card parties, suppers, and fairs. By the fall of 1927, they had raised $2,000 and with it purchased the doughboy statue, which was presented to the borough on Armistice Day, 1927. The elm trees in the park were also donated by the auxiliary, while the first flag to be unfurled from the flag pole in the park was given by the Junior Order of United American Mechanics. The park continues to evolve. Two weeping willows were dedicated on May 30, 1932 in tribute to George Washington as part of the national activities commemorating Washington's 200th anniversary. During World War II, the park was the site of the borough's honor roll. A sundial was placed in Memorial Park by the Women's Club in memory of Elizabeth S. (Clark) Clegg, the only woman from Matawan to serve overseas in World War I. A memorial to local firemen was later added to the park, as was a black granite memorial wall bearing the names of all borough residents in military service during wartime from World War II to the Persian Gulf War.

One of the most memorable events of the first quarter of the twentieth century occurred in late 1918 when T.A. Gillispie and Company, a shell-loading depot at Morgan, went up in a series of thunderous explosions at 7:36 p.m. Alerted by the rumbling and shaking of their homes, and the sound of windows shattering and

One of two fire companies that formed in 1903, the M.E. Haley Company, purchased a motor-driven chemical truck in 1918 at a cost of $2,575, most of which was raised by subscription.

plaster cracking, residents of Matawan and Keyport who were employed at the plant tried to reach the site to help in combating the flames. Accounts reported, "the roads were soon choked with cars rushing to aid the victims" and, "There was scarcely a family that remained in its home in Keyport or Matawan." The violent explosions rocked buildings and National Guardsmen detailed from Red Bank ordered residents from their houses. In Matawan, as well as neighboring Keyport, the schools and other public spaces were opened to the people and straw was spread on the floors to provide bedding. Plant officials estimated 100 people were killed in the explosions. (At the time, the area was in the midst of a major influenza epidemic, so additional deaths could be attributed to the Morgan explosion as many sick people left their homes only to contract pneumonia.)

Over the course of the town's history, the citizens have formed organizations in response to disasters of various kinds. Many of them have grown and are still active in the twenty-first century. Two years after the great fire of 1901, M.E. Haley Hose Company was to join the list of fire companies. Michael E. Haley was the prime mover in the organizing of the company that bears his name. Other early members were Charles E. Close, William A. Kennedy, John Haley, and Elwood VanBrakle. The company purchased a motor-driven chemical truck in 1918 at a cost of $2,575, most of which was raised by subscription.

The firehouse for the M.E. Haley Hose Company was on Main Street near the railroad. The Midway Hose Company was another to form in 1903 and was originally on Washington Street before relocating to Broad Street. Years later, a major contribution of the company was its response to the fire that destroyed the Graf Hindenburg at Lakehurst.

The area's fire protection expanded in 1921 with the formation of the Freneau Independent Fire Company. In an accounting of fire departments for the period 1910 to 1913 in *The Matawan Journal*, Chief Charles R. Stryker reported the following: Levitt Manufacturing Company, Church Street, total loss; Frank Anderson Basket Factory, Atlantic Avenue, total loss; and Matawan Iron and Steel, sparks from locomotive caused minor damage. Industries were not the only places where fires occurred; 13 other fires occurred in small businesses or homes from causes such as defective chimneys, overheated oil stoves, overheated stove pipes, or in the case of John Mulsoff of Main Street, explosion of a motorcycle that damaged the bathroom of the house.

With the United States involved in World War I and the nearby Morgan disaster fresh in their minds, a group of civic-minded citizens met in the Maple Place (then known as Mott Street), Keyport workshop of Thomas E. Kearney, and the Oak Shades Fire Company No. 1, now known as the Aberdeen Township Hose and Chemical Company, was organized in late 1918. Within a month, a lot had been purchased on Lower Main Street. A firehouse was erected on the site, and

Two years after the great fire of 1901, Midway Hose Company joined the list of Matawan's fire companies.

by late 1922 the company purchased its first motorized equipment, a Seagrave pumper, from the City of Long Branch, New Jersey. Sometime after 1932, the original wooden firehouse burned and the records of the Ladies Auxiliary were lost or destroyed. The company built a new brick firehouse on Lower Main on the corner of Gerard Avenue in 1951 and is now housed in a modern firehouse built in 1968 at 490 Lloyd Road.

The biggest changes in the 1920s came to the township in the form of a major development as two developers, Charles W. Morrisey and Samuel W. Walker, bought land in the Cliffwood Beach section of the township. Originally marketed to New York City dwellers, the first lots were sold for both country and seashore summer homes, or as a location for year-round homes. A postcard for the firm advertised a complete four-room home selling for as low as $1,690 with a $100 cash down payment and $18.12 a month. Small summer bungalows were being sold for $585 and "little" farms within a mile of the beach for $600. Although the layout of the streets in Cliffwood Beach may appear haphazard today, *The Matawan Journal* explained there were several reasons for the original layout: "The layout of the streets at Cliffwood Beach will be unique for this section of the county. Practically every lot will have a vista different from all other lots. This combined with the curvilinear streets, breaks up the monotony of parallel streets with houses set in rows."

It was also planned that all traffic would flow through the geographic center of the community. Although Morrisey and Walker did the major development of Cliffwood, they did not build all the homes there. In the 1850s, Henry L. Clarke of New York purchased land to develop as a shore resort, but sold fewer than 20 lots. Clarke's daughter is attributed with naming the area Cliffwood.

With the influx of population came the need for additional services. The Cliffwood Grade School was erected in 1912 at a cost of $6,870. Since it replaced a former district schoolhouse built before 1854, it became the oldest site in the Matawan-Aberdeen district continuously used for education. Less than ten years later, four additional rooms were added at a cost of $23,471 for general contractor, $3,682 heating and ventilation, $200 electrical, and $350 plumbing. There were 48 pupils in Cliffwood when the original building was erected. Matawan High School was built in 1923 at a cost of $149,595. The first traffic light in the township was erected in 1930 at the intersection of Cliffwood Avenue and Route 35. The Civic Association, which had been formed in 1922, was instrumental in securing it.

One of the most visible local landmarks for many years was the pirate ship. While more recent residents may remember the brightly-painted ship, they may not know that the ship actually "sailed up and down" the highway several times. Used by Morrisey & Walker, Inc. for their real estate office, the ship was originally situated in Cliffwood at Shore Concourse and Amboy Avenue. Over the years, the ship was moved up to Laurence Harbor when development was being done there. Then it traveled back down Route 35 and moored in Cliffwood Beach on the northbound side at Raritan Boulevard (where the 7-11 convenience store later

The Cat 'n Fiddle, the Casino, and beach access were among the draws to Cliffwood Beach during its heyday as a summer resort in the 1920s and 1930s.

was built). It was then moved across the street to the southbound side to moor at Greenwood Drive. Of course, since it was not a real ship, the sailing up and down the highway was done by truck, not by sail.

The development of Cliffwood consisted of more than just houses. Jetties and bulkheads were built in 1924, as well as a mile-long boardwalk, bathhouses, and lockers. In 1926, the Country Club was built near the southerly end of the boardwalk at the edge of Treasure Lake. It had wide verandas and an esplanade on the opposite side of the boardwalk. The Cat 'n Fiddle restaurant was built that same year at the north end of the boardwalk. The Cliffwood Beach Pool was started in 1928 and completed the following year. At one time, it was described as "one of the outstanding salt water swimming pools along the coast."

A swimming world record was set at the pool's opening when Rutgers University alumnus George Kojac, an Olympic gold medalist and the world's record backstroke champion, broke his previous record for the 100-yard distance by 1.4 seconds. Johnny Weissmuller, who was Kojac's teammate in the 400-meter freestyle relay at the 1928 Olympics, also swam at the Cliffwood Pool. Weissmuller, the American freestyle swimmer of the 1920s who won five Olympic gold medals and set 67 world records, is perhaps best known for his role as Tarzan in 16 movies. Also in 1928, two large concession buildings were erected—one for refreshments and the other for an arcade with skee ball and bowling. The following year, a recreation park was built with two miniature golf courses and hardball and tennis courts. In the last few decades of the twentieth century, the 1,000-foot beach area was rebuilt by the township as part of a beach protection project begun in 1980. An over 100-acre township-maintained park

Among the special events held on the boardwalk at Cliffwood and in the borough were baby parades and beauty pageants. In this 1936 parade, the 250th anniversary of Matawan's founding, first prize for the float, baby carriage, and express wagon divisions was $10 or equivalent in merchandise.

with tennis, basketball, bocce ball, shuffleboard, and beach access replaced the 1920s amusements.

Along with development came other changes. St. Marks African Methodist Episcopal Zion Church in Cliffwood was founded in 1925 by Reverend Edward Wortham. The members adopted the name Union AME Church, but later changed it to St. Marks AME Zion Church after the congregation obtained a charter from the AME Zion Conference in 1928. Meetings were first held in a tent until a small wood frame building was erected using donated materials with members of the congregation providing the work force. In 1938, plans were made and work begun on a cinder block church on Delaware and Bayview Avenues in Cliffwood. Over the years, additional lots were acquired, a church parsonage built, and the church building expanded and renovated.

The Providence Baptist Church in Cliffwood Beach was originally part of the Mt. Moriah Baptist Church, but was incorporated as a separate congregation in 1927 by Reverend and Mrs. Smith. A story was told about the early days of the church when the building had no pews. Members sat on chairs brought from home and the church was heated by an old wood and coal pot-bellied stove. Reverend B.B. Burgess was the congregation's first pastor.

The Cliffwood Angels Field Camp was organized in 1934 with the goal of seeing that the young children would not have to beg for baseballs or bats, and would have a place to play without being chased, as were the founding members of the group. According to a township history, "The club house was anyone's garage." The 30 to 40 members held ball games and boxing events. Inactive during World War II while most of the members were in the service, the group became active again after the servicemen returned. For the period 1945 to 1950, club members played semi-professional football, baseball, and other sports. Over the years, the club took over a township Little League team, and within three years won the Bayshore Championship. For a time, the club also sponsored a yearly Halloween parade in the township. The former Center Avenue was renamed Angels Street in honor of the club. The Cliffwood Angels were not the only such group in the township at the time. The Cliffwood Royals Social and Athletic Club was organized in 1946 to provide athletic and social activities for the boys in the Cliffwood area and to build a club for recreational purposes for the young people of the community. The group organized its first baseball team in 1946. Both the Angels and the Royals were still active in 1961 and were listed in a local directory.

When the Cliffwood Volunteer Fire Company No. 1 was incorporated in the summer of 1927, it had already purchased equipment—a one-ton Dodge Graham

In the early twentieth century, baseball was a popular pastime with both sexes. Some teams were sponsored by area factories and ceased to exist when the factories closed. This image shows the women's baseball team in 1907. "Heinie" Zimmerman, famous slugging infielder for the Chicago Cubs and New York Giants, and winner of the baseball Triple Crown, played with the Matawan town team in 1906.

truck with a 150-gallon pumping apparatus, 80-gallon booster tank, and 500 feet of 2.5-inch hose—which they housed in Thomas Ryan's garage on Route 35 until a firehouse was built. Ryan helped provide the land and George Craigen, owner of Craigen Brick Company in Cliffwood, donated brick for a firehouse, which was completed the following year. Over the years, the unit's trucks were upgraded, and in 1947 they had the modern necessity of two-way radios.

Cliffwood's first fire alarm was a railroad tire iron placed on the Regan property on Route 35. Later, Keyport's Eagle Hose Company loaned the company a bell they were to use for many years. As the area developed a need for a modern alarm system, the Cliffwood company raised funds, and early in 1934 a Gamewell alarm was installed on the 60-foot tower in the rear of the firehouse. Eventually, a button was installed in the home of Frank and Mary Raffa to sound the alarm so the Raffas would not have to run to the firehouse and sound it manually.

For many years, the fire companies of the borough and the township were a single fire department. One explanation given in local lore for the 1876 breaking away of the borough firemen from the township is that the Matawan Fire Company, which consisted of volunteers, was called to a fire in Cliffwood. The company had to pull the apparatus all the way by manpower. Water had to be secured by suctioning from streams and lakes and by bucket brigades. On this

The first firehouse for the Cliffwood Volunteer Fire Company was built in 1928. In 1955, the Board of Fire Commissioners approved the construction of an addition to the original firehouse, both of which remained in use until 1981 when the building was demolished and a new firehouse built in its place.

John G. Deckert was not only the stationmaster at the Cliffwood station (shown here), but was also the first postmaster at the Cliffwood Post Office.

particular call, despite all their effort, the house was not saved and burned to the ground. The company expected the customary donation, but according to the story, the owner "refused to give them a dime." The incident was supposed to have so angered the volunteers that they voted to break away from the township.

Like the borough, Cliffwood was a stop on the railroad and was briefly called Hutschler's Crossing. However, unlike the station in Matawan-Aberdeen, which remains one of the busiest on the line, it is no longer a stop. Although the station agent was removed in 1931, the Cliffwood station continued as a stop on the New York & Long Branch line until the late 1960s. When the Cliffwood Post Office was established in the winter of 1885, John G. Deckert was not only the first postmaster, but he also served as the agent at the Cliffwood railway station. The post office is no longer in the small wooden building by the tracks, but in a modern brick building in the A&P shopping center on Route 35 and Cliffwood Avenue.

Cliffwood was not the only development in the 1920s as Matawan became home to two lakes. The creation of a lake at Matawan had been under consideration since 1914. Early in 1916, a lake committee was formally incorporated with Tunis R. Schenck as president; H.C. Higgins, vice-president; Ira Sheppard, secretary; and Christian Heuser, treasurer. Shares were sold at $1 each and the subscription list was placed every Saturday evening in George Heuser's barbershop at 188 Main Street. The amount of $1,500 was raised and permission was obtained from the War Department to change the course of Gravelly Creek to the north side of the ravine and to make a dam. In late spring 1923, the valve in the Main

Street dam was shut and the lake began to fill. Within a week, the first rowboat was launched on Lake Matawan by impatient townspeople. In less than a month, water splashed over the dam. At the time, Lake Matawan was 300 feet wide. It backed past the Little Street Bridge to Church Street, and beyond the filtering plant of the borough's water system. According to the town's 1936 history, "The maximum depth of 16 feet was more than enough for divers, and the shore line was sufficiently regular to please young men and women fond of paddling canoes by the light of the moon." Although the lake still exists, due to silting resulting from development during the 1960s, it only reaches to Little Street and has lost most of its recreational allure.

Although Lake Matawan is not what it once was, Matawan still has facilities for water recreation. A few years after Lake Matawan was finished, local attention turned to Matawan Creek, which had lost out as the site of the first dam. Subscription books were opened again to raise $15,000. As it was a bull market on Wall Street, the lake committee was able to raise funds for another dam. By October 1929 the lake, which was named after Jacob R.V. Lefferts who led much of the effort, was overflowing its dam. Lake Lefferts was approximately 1 mile long and 300 to 600 feet wide. The lake is used for boating, swimming, and an annual fireworks display, and is home to an occasional snapping turtle. Although turtles are no longer a common sight near local lakes and wetlands, they can still be found. A large snapping turtle was sighted in the backyard of the Burrowes Mansion in the summer of 2001. As late as the 1950s, children who lived near Lake Lefferts were told to be wary of snapping turtles. Snapping turtles are not the acquiescent box turtles some had as children. The snapping turtles had nasty tempers, fast reflexes, and could bite off fingers if they got too close. Some residents remember turtles being caught and eaten by some local residents.

A local tradition centering around the lake is the closing of Ravine Drive for residents to gather at the dam and the recreational area to witness the Fourth of July fireworks display. According to the 1936 history of the town and recollections of local residents, for a time the lake provided its own pyrotechnical displays. As the story is recounted, on a January Day in 1934, a skater tossed a lit cigarette into an air hole on the ice-covered lake. The resultant flames that flared up from the hole amused the skaters, who joined in on the sport, starting bonfires at every airhole. When Lake Lefferts was formed, not all the vegetable matter was removed. The pyrotechnical displays were caused by gas formed from the decaying vegetable matter in the lakebed. Even in later years, gas bubbles could be seen by swimmers.

6. CHANGING TIMES

Although the period of the 1930s to the 1950s started off with the Great Depression, it can still be called Matawan's most industrial period. World War II in the 1940s and the Korean War in the 1950s were other major concerns of local residents as the town and township continued on its development toward becoming the area familiar to today's residents. Back then, anniversary notices appeared on the front page and the paper carried local news, including birthday parties held, vacations taken, and who had weekend guests. Even minor accidents appeared in the paper, such as a Matawan physician treating a local teenager for leg injuries after the sled she was riding crashed into a tree.

Another illustration of the times is shown by the prices in a 1936 advertisement for Bell Beef. Veal sold for 23¢ per pound; Philadelphia scrapple, 10¢ per pound; and choice grade sirloin steak, 25¢ per pound. Coal, which was still a popular fuel by which to heat homes, could be purchased at a rate of $11.75 per ton. The borough first aid squad, composed of active and exempt firemen, was formed in 1933. The following year, the unit was one of those that responded to an all-county call-out to aid victims of the S.S. *Morro Castle* when it burned off Belmar, New Jersey and eventually drifted ashore near the Convention Hall in Asbury Park.

For many people living in Matawan and Aberdeen in the late twentieth century, the term Prohibition brings to mind Chicago in the 1920s with Elliot Ness and his Untouchables, and Al Capone. Due to the access to waterways and closeness to New York City, both the borough and the township had their own version of the gangster scene complete with federal raids, midnight rendevous, and moonshiners. In October 1933, as the country was voting to end Prohibition, federal agents raided a small farm at the head of Lake Lefferts, seizing and dismantling a still valued at $25,000. Although occupied by transients when it burned in late 1931, the Woodbine Hotel (built by John H. Farry in 1891) was at one time an area landmark. When William Kennedy Sr. and Jr. operated the hotel, the lower floor of the building was padlocked by the federal government for violation of the Prohibition Act.

Only days after 1934 began, federal agents descended on the former Joseph Fisher Bag and Burlap Company. The large, 50-by-100-foot brick building at the

Although taken in the 1950s, the gravel-covered road of Dock Street evokes images of bootleg whiskey-making and Prohibition.

foot of Dock Street, on the dividing line between the borough and the township, was being used for the bootleg production of alcohol. Found in it were seventeen 1,250-gallon cypress tanks or vats for fermentation. The local paper reported the use of only pure grain and sugar and "only the purest alcohol was run." Atlantic Avenue residents reported that, for some months prior to the raid, auto traffic had been exceedingly heavy; trucks were making frequent visits to the site between 1 a.m. and 3 a.m.; and before the creek froze, motor boats were plying to and from the bulkhead, which was 75 feet from the building. In late December that same year, a raid in Cliffwood uncovered a 2,500-gallon still in a home on South Concourse. In the summer of 1938, two men were taken into custody for possession of a still on Bayview Avenue in Cliffwood.

Perhaps the most interesting raid took place not in a secluded rural or industrial area, but in the middle of town on Little Street in the rear of William M. Smith's blacksmith shop in November 1934. At the time, it was reported that the bootlegging operation would not have been found, except there was a fire in the one-room concrete building caused by fumes igniting when the firebox was opened. The fumes were supposedly so strong because so much effort had been taken in closing and covering all windows and other openings to conceal the illicit operations that the plant was improperly ventilated. At the time of the fire, the plant was believed to have been in operation from ten days to two weeks. According to officials at the time, that type of illegal cracking plant could produce 1,000 gallons daily at a profit of $1 per gallon. With the usual lifetime of ten days before discovery and abandonment, such plants could make $10,000 before the operators moved onto another site.

One of the most unusual stories of the time was the shooting of Patrolman John J. Flood. Flood was critically wounded in the head by a masked invader in Matawan police headquarters on June 18, 1934. What is unusual about the story is that headlines in the February 7, 1936 issue of *The Matawan Journal* stated that Flood showed improvement after coughing up the bullet. What makes the story more unusual is that the bullet was supposedly coughed up two years after the original shooting. Flood would later work his way up to chief of police.

In 1929, the bottom dropped out of the stock market, ushering in the Great Depression, the worst economic crisis in United States history. The Great Depression had an effect on local residents beyond plant closures, as Matawan Bank closed in December 1931 to protect its depositors. The local paper reported that in March 1935, a resolution was presented to the Matawan Township Committee seeking a relief grant of $6,300 from the state and $250 from the township for the month of March. At the time, the township had 234 families with 940 people on relief out of a possible 2,200 people.

Although the major development of the township was not to occur for several more decades, as early as 1938, new residents were being encouraged to move to Aberdeen. Many of the amenities of the current township can be seen in the following 1938 advertisement, as well as several items that have ceased to exist:

> In the township you will find Municipal water, approved schools, police radio cars, improved roads, ample police reserve, rail and bus facilities, organized fire protection, only 26 miles to New York, low commutation rates to the metropolitan area; low taxes, yacht basins, 3 fine lakes, summer cottages, rich farming land, modern home developments, bathing/boating/fishing/skating; largest salt water pool in the Bayshore.

A visiting nurse serviced the township (municipality) for a nominal fee through the cooperation of the Matawan Public Health Association. The area received a modern post office with the April 1938 dedication of a new building at 155 Main Street.

A January 1936 issue of *The Matawan Journal* had a story on a topic that should sound familiar to many later township residents: the paper reported that bids were authorized at a township meeting to lay transmission water mains in Cliffwood and Oak Shades to be financed by the Federal Emergency Administration of Public Works. Only in later years, the issue of township water service focused more on Freneau.

Boundary lines between the borough and township have been changed twice since their original conception. A bill was introduced into the state legislature in the spring of 1931 for the annexation of a part of Freneau, for land adjoining Lake Lefferts, and land between Lake Matawan and Atlantic Avenues into the borough. A special election was held later that spring for those affected by the annexation. The vote for annexation was carried by 17 votes. *The Matawan Journal* reported that the land area to be added was more than two times larger than the land area of the borough at the time, but added less than 150 people to the population. The following year, *The Matawan Journal* had the headline "Freneau May Seek Annexation to the Boro of Matawan—Not Satisfied with the Township Proposition." This second annexation of Freneau land was decided in May 1933 when it was approved with a vote of 66 to 51. Of a possible 124 votes, 117 were cast.

According to the 1936 history of Matawan, the Matawan station was a busy one on the Central Railroad of New Jersey, and at the time, the town had an estimated

In 1875, The Matawan Journal *commented on the arrival of the railroad: "The 'Keyport Weekly' charges that people from Matawan 'paid $100,000 to bend the railroad line to suit her purposes and avoiding the straight line which would have accommodated Keyport.'" They then commented that they were guaranteed 7 percent per year on the money spent. Matawan Railroad Station is shown here in 1906.*

Although there are no longer any new car dealerships in the borough or the township, there have been many over the years where Fords and Pontiacs, Overlands and Packards were sold. Mount Barrett Ford, shown here, was on Main Street during the 1930s and 1940s.

commuting population of 300. In 2000, the station was the busiest one on the North Jersey Coast Line with an estimated 3,400 commuters using the station. Another illustration of how times have changed was that when the Matawan station opened in 1875, horse and buggies were a popular way to get to the train and the yearly commutation cost to New York City was $100. Automobiles have since replaced the horse and buggy. According to the *Asbury Park Press* in February 2002, there were almost 1,400 parking spaces between the borough and township for commuters using the North Jersey Coast Line. Another station, long since closed, stood on Stillwell Street.

Not everyone commuted by train. In 1916, the local paper advertised that you could buy an Overland Model 75 for $615 from Bushnell's Garage. According to 1936 editions of *The Matawan Journal*, there were several automobile dealers in the town. Located on Main Street were Stricklands at 114 Main, Pontiacs; Dick Lambertson at 182 Main Street, Buicks and Packards; and Mount Barrett at 60 Main Street, Fords, Fordsons, and Lincolns. Leslie Lines and Amos B. Stultz were proprietors of the Jackson Street Garage where they sold Plymouths at 172 Jackson Street. A 1937 advertisement stated that you could buy from them "The Glamour car of 1938—the Big Beautiful New Jubilee Plymouth." Mueller Chevrolet was a staple on Route 34 in the 1960s. Although Tom's Ford later moved to Route 35 in Keyport, the 1963 *Matawan Journal* contained an advertisement for the company, which at the time was selling Fords in the former Mount Barrett showroom. In the 1960s and 1970s, Bill Lanzaro sold Simcas, Fiats, and Sunbeams from a showroom on the corner of Main Street and Route 516. Several dealerships sold Chevrolets and Oldsmobiles out of 110 Main Street, including Thixtons (1930s to 1950s); Johnson-Gibb (1960s); and Steven Oldsmobile (early 1970s). Downes

Pontiac was a mainstay in the Oak Shades section for many years before closing down in the 1970s. As the borough approached the twenty-first century, there were no longer new car dealerships in either the township or the borough. Most of the once-familiar dealership names were no longer in business. To illustrate changes in prices, in 1936, a car could be purchased for $990 to $1,115 at the Buick Packard dealership. In 2002, $16,997 was required to buy a Pontiac Grand Prix SE.

One purpose of histories is to show similarities between times past and present. Under the heading of "some things never change," in the January 17, 1936 edition of *The Matawan Journal*, it was reported that the Matawan Borough Police Department was determined to put an end to speeding and reckless driving within borough limits, and had issued 20 summonses since January 1. In the same timeframe, there were 42 accidents in the borough. Similar sentiments about reckless and speeding drivers were echoed many years later. Accidents were not the only problem for car owners. The January 3, 1936 *Matawan Journal* reported on a Middlesex County car theft ring in which four brothers, including one who lived in Cliffwood, were arrested. It also reported that the Perth Amboy police recovered 12 stolen cars.

The Aberdeen Township Police Department was organized in 1935. Originally, the two-man force worked 12-hour shifts without a day off until J. Edgar Wilkinson was appointed as special officer in 1939 and assigned to work weekends to allow the regulars a day off. In 1957, the department consisted of the chief, captain, 4 patrolmen, 45 special police, and 2 radio-controlled cruiser cars. By 1993, the township law enforcement department had grown to 28 officers, 13 vehicles, with total operational costs of $2,170,011.

During the 1930s, Matawan Borough, and to a lesser extent the township, remained an industrial area until World War II caused many of the firms to close. Few reminders of most of the companies remain although they were major employers at the time. Among those missing from the later twentieth-century landscape were Charles E. Walling's Monmouth Stamping Company, which specialized in making electric stoves and electric shades. The firm was started on Atlantic Avenue in 1930. A 1936 *Matawan Journal* advertisement reported the firm, operating out of an 1,800-square-foot main building and 1,000-square-foot circular steel storage shed, could turn out 400 stoves daily. It was also during this time that the area was known for its chicken farms. March Farms advertised that they were "the farm that made and introduced Jersey Giants to America," and that they offered both black and white Jersey Giants.

The noise and light of a meteorite that streaked over Matawan in the spring of 1936 had many area residents recalling the harrowing experiences of the famed Morgan explosion. The local paper reported that residents thought that the boilers in their own or adjoining homes had exploded, and that other townspeople were equally sure that an industrial plant in Perth Amboy or some nearby manufacturing section had been destroyed by a blast. Local residents described the passage of a "white ball of fire traveling like a shooting star at a terrific rate across the sky," accompanied by a thundering noise. Fragments of a meteorite were later found in Red Bank, Highland Park, and Spring Lake. Ten years later, local residents felt and heard another explosion when the chemical drying tower at the Endurette Corporation of America's block-long factory in Cliffwood was leveled by fire following an explosion in the tower that was felt and heard for more than 2 miles. Three employees were killed and four others seriously injured in the explosion and fire that caused damage unofficially estimated at $500,000. Endurette Corporation manufactured waterproofed fabrics.

The meteorite was not Matawan's only tie to the skies. A Matawan firm contributed to the setting of a 1938 world record when a small Piper Cub powered by a 50-horsepower Lenape "Papoose" engine flew non-stop between Newark Airport and Miami and back. The Papoose was designed by Joseph Boland, owner of the Lenape Aircraft and Motors, Inc. of Matawan, which built the engine. The flight was to prove that light aircraft of the day were not just toys. As it was impossible for the plane to fly that distance without refueling, a unique in-air refueling technique was used. At specified airports along its route, the Cub was brought down within 15 feet of the runway. Then, flying steadily

The Matawan Borough Police Department was established in 1927 with two members. By 2001, the department had increased to 11 vehicles and 22 officers, including K-9 Officer Wolf and his handler Officer Patrick Walker.

113

Contrasting the Eastern Airliner and the Piper Cub, pilots Kenny Kress and Glenn Englert plot the course for their 1938 record-setting trip. Using 223 gallons of gas and 25 quarts of oil, the plane flew continuously for two and a half days, making a non-stop round trip between Newark, New Jersey and Miami, Florida.

at that height, a rope was dropped from the plane to a car speeding along below. Five-gallon cans of gas were tied to the rope as the plane and car sped along a parallel route at more than 50 miles per hour. At each airport, the procedure was repeated five or six times until 30 gallons were lifted aboard the plane. The Piper Cub landed back at Newark some 63 hours and 55 minutes after it had departed, establishing a new distance record for small aircraft of 2,420 miles on a point-to-point basis.

With his brother Frank, Boland flew the first fixed wing aircraft in New Jersey in November 1909. While working for the Aeromarine Plane and Motor Company of Keyport, he designed and built a small 45-horsepower, 3-cylinder radial type, air-cooled engine known as the Papoose. At the same time, he was also operating his own personal machine shop in Matawan. In 1930, James Helme took over the manufacturing rights of the Papoose engine as well as Joseph's shop, and formed Lenape Aircraft and Motors, Inc. Boland joined Helme and they operated a small engine business for commercial aircraft until World War II.

It was also during the 1930s that the Burrowes Mansion again returned to being a public house as Thora Thomsen rented the mansion and operated the Colonial Tea House. The tea house celebrated its grand opening on Friday, March 15, 1935 and was run for three years until Mildred Brown (one of B.F.S. Brown's daughters) decided to come home to stay. The Colonial Tea House served luncheon and dinner, catered to private parties, and set up tables for impromptu bridge games for those enjoying the pastime. Lunches were priced 35¢ to 50¢; dinners ranged from 50¢ to $1. In *The Burrowes Mansion of Matawan, N.J.,* the experience was described as follows: "Patrons dined amidst antiques, and those seated in the original dining room could gaze through the windows and enjoy the lovely flower gardens, in season, in the rear of the house." On June 1, 1938, the heirs of B.F. S. Brown conveyed the property at 94 Main Street to Mildred Brown Herrick and her husband Ralph Waldo Herrick.

In January 1935, the fire departments were kept busy with four fires within a 24-hour period. At the home of Mr. and Mrs. Rubin Lunt on Dock Street, seven-year-old Cliestra Carpenter was awakened by the family dog Queen. The child sounded the alarm and everyone escaped. The house burnt to the ground, but the neighboring industrial buildings were not damaged. A fire on New Years night that gutted the Lower Main Street house of Mr. and Mrs. Michael Tomisello was said to have been caused by an overheated stove. One interesting fact about one of the other fires is that it occurred at the home of Antonio Scully on Kane Terrace (now Highfield Avenue in Aberdeen); Scully, a member of the M.E. Haley Hose Company, was out fighting another fire at the time.

Pearl Harbor was the beginning of fearful times marked by acceleration of the draft, rationing, war news, casualties, and stalking, naked fear. Throughout World War II, there was the very real fear that the enemy might rain bombs on the local communities. *The Matawan Journal* described local conditions, including blackouts, air raid drills, shore patrols, and aircraft warning stations. However, at least before atomic fission and the dropping of atomic bombs on Hiroshima and Nagasaki, they were not haunted by the fear that the war would end in the destruction of civilization.

After the United States joined the fight in 1941, the local draft board went into action to call to the colors every able bodied young man in the vicinity. Over the next four years, many local young men boarded the train at Matawan Station to go off to war and their names were recorded on large rolls of honor. When the 1943 Matawan High School graduation exercises were held, four of the 70 graduates were already in the military service and missed the commencement exercises. The class motto, "Impossible is Un-American," reflected the attitude of the times.

115

The Matawan Journal described the cost of the war to the nation as more than 1.25 million boys killed, wounded, or missing, leaving homes by the thousands with one or more family members gone. The 1945 Victory edition of *The Matawan Journal* listed almost 200 local men in military service during World War II. A number of those who went off to war never returned, including six township men: Robert H. Bennett, William T. Cross, George T. Durante, Charles Anthony Kaleda, John James Short, and William Frank Starkey Jr. Among those lost with ties to the borough were Spafford W. Schanck Jr., Luke J. Durante, Emilio A. Parisi, Wilbur McElvaine, John H. Winschuh, William L. Dernberger, John Guigliano, and Arris Gordon Banke. Banke died in April 1942 in a training accident in Florida over the Gulf of Mexico. McElvaine died at Guadalcanal in September 1942 while attempting to secure help for his unit surrounded by Japanese.

The loss of local manpower to military service during World War II affected the local area in other ways. One example was the necessity of an acting chief while the township police chief served in the navy. Thomas J. Sinnett filled in for the police chief, Thomas F. Powers, D.D.S., during his term of service. Fire departments were shorthanded due to members in service. In some cases, several members of the same family were in service at the same time, such as Vincent Tomasello and three of his brothers. Tomasello was awarded the Bronze Star medal for "meritorious achievement in connection with military operations" at Aitape, New Guinea, during late 1944. World War II touched the Baptist congregation in a very personal way when their pastor, Reverend Garrett Detwiler, enlisted in the United States Army and received a commission as a first lieutenant in March 1944. After serving in the European theater, Detwiler returned as pastor to the congregation at the end of the war, serving until 1952.

Men were not the only ones in military service during World War II. The 1957 township history notes Alida E. Vervoort (née Alida Chete), held the distinction of being one of the first women from Matawan Township to enlist. According to the 1957 township history, when Vervoort and 22 other female enlistees from New Jersey reported for duty in October 1942, the service wasn't ready for the women and initially issued them general issue uniforms for men. The women reportedly appeared for a time in oversized coats and hats.

It is interesting to contrast the reaction to and support efforts of local residents during World War II as compared to the indifference more prevalent 20 years later regarding the Vietnamese conflict. During World War II, members of the women's club were air wardens, plane spotters, and Red Cross volunteers. Another major activity of local residents, both young and old, during the war was the purchase of war bonds and stamps. One report by Corporal Marjorie Concepcion, who was in charge of selling war stamps and bonds in the Cliffwood Public School during the 1943–1944 school year, was that the pupils purchased stamps amounting to $687.15. Bonds and stamps sold to the pupils or through their solicitation amounted to $2,346.70. Advertisements in a June 1943 edition of *The Matawan Journal* show that the Matawan Theater was showing "Sergeant York," starring Gary Cooper, and "Casablanca," starring Humphrey Bogart, Ingrid Bergman, and

During World War II, husband and wife Robert and Shirley VanBrakle Bentley pose in uniform before going to their separate posts, with one serving in the Army and the other in the Navy.

Paul Henreid. Comedic relief was provided by the Dead End Kids and the Little Tough Guys in "Mug Town."

Those on the home front were also concerned with the war's impact on the necessities and comforts. They worried about shortages of sugar, coal, gasoline, fly swatters, and the other accoutrements of civilian life. The rationing of gasoline and tires was not the only impediment to driving during the war years. To help conserve gasoline, motor vehicles were restricted to a maximum speed of 35 miles per hour as part of the war effort. In the summer of 1943, Matawan police stopped almost 100 cars on Routes 4 and 34, not as part of a drunk driving roadblock, but as part of the pleasure-driving ban. According to the local paper, the majority of the drivers had letters stating they were going to the hospital to visit friends or relatives. Inspectors of the Office of Price Administration centered the weekend check on highways to the shore and to North Jersey amusement parks, resulting in 279 persons being cited for pleasure driving. During the Matawan stop, the local paper reported what it referred to as an "amusing incident" involving a florist truck from New York. When the rear doors were opened, they "revealed nine passengers camouflaged behind a screen of geraniums." The group had planned to spend the day at the seashore, but were sent back to their homes.

Local industries also contributed to the war effort. One firm that made several significant contributions was Hanson–Van Winkle–Munning. In early 1942, the Japanese forces occupying Malaysia cut off the supply of tin to the United States as part of a plan to render the American war effort ineffectual due to the lack of the metal. Wesley F. Hall, chief design engineer of Hanson–Van Winkle–Munning, drew the attention of the American military when he developed a plating process that significantly reduced the tin resources needed. The new process used only three-quarters of a pound of tin, where 1.25 pounds would have been needed for the same result before the war.

According to a *Matawan Journal* article written 30 years after the war, Hall made another significant contribution to the war effort. Development of the atom bomb had come to a critical halt in 1943 when the scientists working on it could not

Members of the Guadalcanal Post 4745 of the Veterans of Foreign Wars have served their country in times of war and peace. Formed on December 10, 1945, the post was originally headquartered in Matawan. In 1950, the post transferred to Cliffwood where it purchased a lot on Hawthorne Street and Cliffwood Avenue, and erected its headquarters building. This photo was taken Memorial Day, 1965.

find a strip-plating process that would adjust to the complexities of the elements making up the bomb. Hall solved the problem. In the desert of Alamogordo, New Mexico, he set up a strip of one metal, 1 yard wide and 2 miles long, and coated it with another metal to the thickness of 0.004 inch. As a result, the development of the atom bomb moved forward to its eventual conclusion with the dropping of atom bombs on Hiroshima and Nagasaki.

Hall and the engineers at Hanson–Van Winkle–Munning made another contribution, albeit a less significant one, to the war effort. After a German U-boat sank several ships loaded with many tons of canned goods in Halifax harbor, salvaging the material seemed futile. The problem was that the rust would eventually eat through the cans and cause total spoilage. Hall and the engineers of Hanson–Van Winkle–Munning devised a machine to take the rust off the cans and coat them with a protective covering at a rate of 60 cans a minute, thus saving the entire shipment and overcoming a supply crisis. Hall and Hanson–Van Winkle–Munning received a citation at the end of the war for their achievements.

As the 1950s dawned, America was moving into the Eisenhower years. It was "Ozzie and Harriet" time, with the Nelsons setting the image for a modern family. A hurricane in 1950 had already destroyed most of the boardwalk and washed away tons of earth from the cliff. In addition to the neighborhood grocery stores in the 1950s, downtown Matawan had two chain grocery stores, the Acme and the A&P. However, they were not like the modern supermarket grocery stores of the same names of today. Located at 127 Main Street, the Acme Market was housed in the former Matawan Theater and had only 30 by 100 feet of floor space. However, an announcement in the local paper did state, "A large parking lot is in the rear for the convenience of customers."

The smaller stores of the 1950s were convenient as most families went grocery shopping every day. People didn't buy shopping carts full of items, just the staples and what they wanted for dinner that night. Idaho potatoes were not the staple of today's stores. Shoppers specified Freehold potatoes if they wanted the freshest potatoes. Except in the middle of winter when no local crops were available, you didn't buy potatoes from Idaho that had been shipped across the country. Instead, you purchased potatoes that had been grown on one of the many area potato farms.

Another change from the mega-markets of the late twentieth century was the organization of the stores. In the 1940s and 1950s, there were not aisles and aisles of items. Many of the items were on shelves behind the counter. When shopping, customers told the cashier what they wanted. As items were taken down and placed on the counter, the price would be written by hand, usually in pencil, on the bag. Since this was before the days of the modern electronic registers, and the mechanical push-button register popularized by National Cash Register was not always in use, after the order was complete, the cashier would add up the columns of numbers in his head. To ensure accuracy, the numbers would need to be double checked by re-adding them a second time. One local resident told about her own double check. While the cashier was adding up the prices, she would read the list

Among the popular entertainments written about in Marjorie VanBrakle's memoirs was the outdoor movie theater in the summer. Sisters Marjorie and Millicent VanBrakle are shown here riding bikes. (Courtesy of the Bentley family.)

upside down and tally it in her head. She said it saved time because the cashier wouldn't have to do the calculations the second time.

Although the outdoor drive-in movie theaters popular for many years are now mostly just memories of members of the baby boomer generation, outdoor movie viewing was known to earlier residents of the town and township. However, Matawan's outdoor movie theater of 1910 differed greatly from those of the 1950s. Instead of parents being seated comfortably in their cars munching on a hot dog and popcorn while their kids slept in the back seat in their pajamas, Genevieve Donnell, a local civic leader and businesswoman, wrote about sitting outdoors on wooden benches and "fighting off the mosquitoes." The benches were set up in the vacant lot at the rear of 128 Main Street, home for many years to Sandford's Pharmacy, for people to view the silent movies accompanied by piano music. And in case of inclement weather, the piano was moved inside and the show went on.

Outdoors was not the only way that local residents could view the products of the fledgling movie industry. Movies were also shown indoors in the building at 128 Main Street, which was known as the Lyric Theater in 1913 and could seat 350 people. Children could see the four one-reel pictures and an illustrated song for the large sum of 10¢. Over the years, entertainment could also be found at the Rivoli Theater at 127 Main Street. Later renamed the Matawan Theater, it closed in the 1950s. Although there are no longer any theaters in the borough, the

Strathmore Theater on Highway 34 in the township helps serve the entertainment needs of the area.

The 1950s were not always a time of perfect harmony. As American-led United Nations troops fought against the forces of North Korea and China in the first armed conflict of the Cold War, the Korean War (1950–1953) had an impact on Matawan and Aberdeen in several ways. The Cliffwood Royals Social and Athletic Club became inactive during the Korean War when eight of its members went into the service. The 1957 history of Aberdeen Township mentioned a local man, Charles P. Millar, who died during the Korean War. In 1950, local residents who had lived through the 1918 Morgan explosion, were again reminded of that night as South Amboy was again rocked by a mighty ammunition blast when a barge loaded with land mines went up on the evening of May 19 with the loss of more than 30 seamen and dock workers. The nine-member Township Civil Defense Council under Peter C. Vena was organized the following year.

When Reverend Chester A. Galloway began his pastorate of the Presbyterian congregation in 1949, he had no idea of some of the drastic changes in store for the church. New residents were coming into the area, and the church bought the house next door for use as classrooms and offices for the church school. It was not the expansion that remains in the memories of local residents, but the Christmas 1955 fire that destroyed the historic sanctuary. On Christmas Eve, a fire broke out in the house next to the church. Because windows were broken to put out the fire, office equipment, such as typewriter, mimeograph, and salvaged church records, were moved into the church. Among those helping was the arsonist, a member of the congregation who had started the fire.

When the fire alarm again sounded at 6:40 p.m. on Christmas Day, the town turned out to see the Presbyterian Church ablaze. A fire had been set in the room where choir robes and anthem music were stored. Although an attempt was made to save church records, the small room beside the pulpit where they had been placed the night before couldn't be reached. In a showing of community support, neighbor churches and auxiliaries set up coffee lines that operated from the kitchen of the nearby Lloyd home. Local residents brought food from their Christmas tables to serve the volunteer firemen who labored through the cold night. Next day, it was discovered that the small room where the records had been stored on Christmas Eve was untouched. Also in the room were the baptismal font and the Communion set. Discovered in the rubble of the church was a small pulpit Bible, a gift from the Glenwood Mission Band on its 60th anniversary. After reading the Christmas scripture, the Bible had been placed under the pulpit on a shelf which apparently protected it from the flames, although the cover was charred and the pages water soaked. The lecture room was not damaged by fire, but water was so deep that holes were bored through the floor to drain it.

Two years after the fire, the cornerstone was laid for a new sanctuary, not on Main Street, but out on Highway 34. Placed inside the cornerstone was *The Matawan Journal* clippings about the church and the fire; a list of building fund contributors; copies of church records, including deeds and membership; a set of

When the Casino burnt to the ground in 1957, it had already been abandoned for a decade. In its heyday in the 1920s, thousands enjoyed the dancing and cooling bay breezes.

1957 coins and a 1957 $1 bill; a list of ministers; and a history of the church. The following November, the congregation moved into the fellowship hall beneath the sanctuary, as the remainder of the church wasn't finished until the following spring. The congregation also got a new home for its pastor, as Mrs. Helen Terhune Schock and J. Mabel Brown gave the former Koopman homestead to the church. Overlooking Lake Lefferts, the home was built in 1930.

In the borough, 1957 was to begin more than a decade of change and controversy for the congregation of the Methodist Episcopal Church on Main Street. That year, the congregation voted unanimously to change the corporate name of the church, dropping Episcopal to reflect changes in the denomination. More controversial was the decision to purchase the property adjacent to the church for use as classrooms and administrative facilities. Some members of the church were sure that it would be impossible for the congregation to raise the $31,500 needed for the purchase and repairs to the home, while others felt that the purchase would eventually bankrupt the congregation. Nevertheless, the motion was carried and the first of several building programs undertaken. The property, once owned by John Terhune, was purchased from Uffredo and Margaret Edwards and began to be referred to as the Church House by the congregation.

As the decade continued, around the area there were several signs of the upcoming growth and modernization. In the mid-1950s, the Memorial School opened in the borough on the Grammar School site on Broad Street and Church Street. The township's first aid squad was organized on March 4, 1954 by Roy S.

Matthews with $150 capital and a 1931 LaSalle ambulance. The 1957 township history reported that activities for the squad's first year were 393 calls made and 3,134 miles traveled. There were 76 fire calls, 10 accident calls, and 155 emergency transports. An auxiliary was organized shortly after the squad was formed and, on September 18, 1954, the auxiliary won a trophy for having the most members in the line of march at the Matawan First Aid Parade. A station house was built on Amboy Avenue and dedicated in June 1966.

What is now sometimes referred to as the Cliffwood First Aid Squad is not the township's only emergency medical response unit. As a result of the population growth resulting from Strathmore, a group of Strathmore men formed a squad and, in November 1964, ground was broken and a small garage was built behind the Lloyd Road firehouse. Originally members of the then Matawan Township First Aid Squad, the Strathmore group split off in 1970 to form an independent unit with 13 charter members and became known as the South Aberdeen Emergency Medical Services (EMS). A separate building for the squad was dedicated at 260 Church Street on June 2, 1973. Like the Matawan school's piano, which it received free in a newspaper contest, the squad received a brand new, fully equipped ambulance from the state of New Jersey under special circumstances. They received the rig for coordinating a course for the newly state-required emergency medical technician certification. Although EMT training is now the standard, at the time some first aid squads operated under Red Cross rules. It is interesting to note that the first certified EMTs in New Jersey were the members of the South Aberdeen EMS, with Joseph Greco holding certification number 1.

In 1953, as part of the area's Civil Defense program, local emergency personnel participated in Operation Valentine, a mock bombing of the Cliffwood Civic Center, organized by the Matawan Township Civil Defense Council. The council was organized in 1951 with the nine members directed by Peter C. Vena.

When it was completed in 1955, the Garden State Parkway changed the township. It actually cut through and divided the township. In order to build the parkway, a new streambed for Matawan Creek, 3,000 feet long and 75 feet wide, was dug, requiring the excavation of 156,000 cubic yards of material. The stream was moved to provide better foundation sites for the parkway bridges. In June 1957, a new water tank, 5 feet higher than the former tank, was put into service in the township to alleviate the water shortage situation in the Cliffwood area particularly during the summer season. Two changes of even greater impact in Cliffwood were the construction two years later of the A&P supermarket and the Cliffwood Memorial School.

In 1955, a brick building was erected by the Famers and Merchants Bank on the corner of Main Street and Ravine Drive. According to the history of the bank, this new building incorporated heating ducts, musical outlets, heating and lighting systems, drive up windows, and parking facilities "not envisioned in older type banking establishments." Acoustical ceilings replaced the high interiors of the earlier style architecture and the safes and records were placed underground in a reinforced concrete vault because "the directors feel that in these times of modern warfare our country may no longer be free from air attack and the most secure place for the valuables of the public is underground." At the time this history was written, the building is still a bank, although due to a series of mergers, it is no longer the Farmers and Merchants Bank.

Early cars, such as this one seen in the Dietrich Brothers Auto Repair shop, would cause heads to turn if it went up the Garden State Parkway. Back when the picture was taken (c. 1910–1920) the car still turned heads, not because of its age, but because there were so few around. The shop was on the Dietrich family homestead on Church Street. (Courtesy of Marie Dietrich Busch.)

7. SEPARATE AND DIFFERENT

The 1960s and 1970s were a time of radical change, not only on a national scale, but also locally. The area lost many of the descendents of the original settlers. The exploration of outer space began in late 1957 with the launch of *Sputnik I*, continuing with the first manned flight into space by Yuri Gagarin in the spring of 1961 and John Glenn's *Friendship 7* orbital flight the following year. Neil Armstrong became the first man on the moon during the summer of 1969.

An event that had a variety of major impacts on the nation in the late 1960s and early 1970s was the Vietnam War. More than 3 million men went overseas to fight for their country. Unlike the sendoffs for the soldiers of the Civil War and World War I, there were no large public farewells for those going into service during the Vietnam era. The farewells were just private affairs as local residents went off singly or in small groups. The Matawan-Aberdeen area had its own casualties among the more than 58,000 men killed or missing in Vietnam. Before the war ended, three men whose home-of-record was Matawan, were killed in action: Donald Allaway, John Engedal, and Edward Haddock.

After United States troops were sent to support South Vietnam in 1965, Americans followed the Vietnam War on television with day-by-day casualty tallies and photographs on the evening news. By the end of the twentieth century, immediate coverage was possible for major events, such as the explosion during the 1986 launch of the *Challenger* space shuttle. Some events were covered almost around the clock. During the 1960s, with the specter of nuclear war looming, bomb drills at schools were a familiar practice. In the early 1970s, the tenor of the Cold War changed as the two superpowers, the U.S.S.R. and the United States, tried to take steps toward controlling the nuclear arms race—efforts that culminated with the tearing down of the Berlin Wall almost 20 years later.

Industry in the borough and township was changing in these two decades as the large manufacturing plants that had been established near the turn of the century closed down and were replaced by smaller firms. The 1965 borough master plan described industrial use in 1964 as only one small section at the north end of Main Street. In the township, Mosaic Tile closed its plant on Atlantic Avenue in the mid-1960s, and M&T Chemical closed its Matawan plant in 1972, laying off the 200-man workforce.

One significant exception to the plant closings was the building in 1962, by American Can, of a new plant in Cliffwood. The company would become one of the largest employers in Aberdeen Township and was described as the "largest independently owned glass company in the world." At one time, it employed 400 people with a yearly salary and fringe benefits payroll of $21 million. Although first used as a warehouse, the plant was later used to manufacture glass containers. By 1994, it was a six-machine operation producing 2.5 million glass bottles per day for products made by Anheuser Busch, Coca Cola, Pepsi, Snapple, Yoo Hoo, and Coors. The firm was purchased by Midland Glass in 1968 and became its headquarters until March 1, 1984 when Anchor Glass purchased Midland Glass. The plant closed in 1996.

The 1960s and 1970s can be characterized as the period of suburbia, as the township and borough changed from a small town surrounded by farm fields to a modern suburban bedroom community. The 1965 Matawan Borough master plan reported a 36.6 percent increase in population between 1950 and 1960; yet there was almost the same increase in the next five years. According to the 1960 census, the median family income was $7,438. There were 320 families with income exceeding $10,000 and 653 families with incomes between $5,000 to $9,000. Although some farming continued, many of the township's farms, orchards, and woods were changing into housing developments. There were some exceptions. A destination for school class trips was the mink ranch on Highway 34. The

Bucking the trend of plant closings, American Can built a plant in Cliffwood in 1962. It lasted until 1996 when it joined the long list of the area's closed manufacturing plants. The American Can production line is shown here in 1965.

The township was not the only area to develop. Church Street, as seen in this early twentieth-century photocard, bears little resemblance to that of the twenty-first.

Fairlawn Acres Farm on Van Brackle Road not only sold eggs and poultry, but advertised that "we deliver." Illustrating the times, Flo's Bar and Grill on Central Avenue promoted that they had television.

Township residents voted in November 1964 to change the committee form of government that had been in effect since 1857. Under the Faulkner Act, the township became one of four municipalities in the state to adopt a council-manager governing format. Under this form of government, the elected seven-member council, of which the mayor is a voting member, appoints a full-time professional manager to direct the day-to-day operations of the township. According to Henry Arnold, a member of the original 1966 council, the switch was made to help deal with the area's burgeoning population, which went from approximately 7,000 people in 1960 to more than 17,000 in 1980.

The change in government was not the only political change in the 1960s and 1970s as residents of Matawan Township voted to change the name of the township. When Philip N. Gumbs was sworn in on January 2, 1974 as mayor of Matawan Township, he was Monmouth County's first African-American mayor. In November 1977, the decision was made that Matawan Township would become Aberdeen Township. No longer would it be "the Matawans," but two separate and distinct identities. There were several reasons for the change, among them confusion between the borough and the township. A State Department of Labor and Industry report listing 455 businesses in the township and the borough, incorrectly credited 76 township businesses to the borough, and 24 borough businesses to the township. Officials also believed the new name would draw attention to the township, as it is listed first alphabetically among New Jersey's 566 municipalities. More importantly, it recalls the origin of the early Scotch settlers who called their community New Aberdeen.

Feelings between the governing bodies of the borough and the township have not always been amicable and cooperative. Illustrating the extent of hostile feelings between borough and township at various points over the years, in 1939, *The Matawan Journal* reported on Mayor C.E. Heuser as he advanced theories for increasing the territory of the borough by doing away with the township: Cliffwood would form a borough of its own; Oak Shades would go with Keyport; and the country section of the township would go to Holmdel. While that particular plan did not go through, over the years there were several annexations of township land by the borough. Matawan Borough's original formation by the incorporation of a part of Matawan Township left some curious anomalies in the boundary lines between the two municipalities. This was further complicated by the Garden State Parkway, which follows a line cutting back and forth across the common boundary. Roughly 350 acres in the township were isolated from the rest by an intervening section of the borough. Another anomaly is a lot on Middlesex Road that is completely within the township, although the rest of the street is part of the borough. The jog was made in deference to the owner, Lewis H. Stemler, the chairman at the time of the Matawan Township Committee (a position that was later officially designated as mayor). The boundary line between the township and the borough splits a home on Mohawk Drive between the two municipalities.

The impetus for many of the changes in the 1960s and early 1970s was the building of Strathmore-at-Matawan, William J. Levitt's fourth large housing venture. Between 1962 and 1964, 1,900 houses were built in ten sections off a 2.5-mile stretch of Lloyd Road. One local resident remembers Lloyd Road before Strathmore as a dirt road. At Strathmore's beginning, there were 48 houses in the middle of orchards and fields. Unlike the bungalows built by Morrisey & Walker, Inc., the Strathmore homes were more spacious, about 1,500 to 1,800 square feet, on lots ranging in size from 7,700 to 11,000 square feet. Each home had a one- or two-car attached garage and air conditioning. The original cost of the homes varied. Depending on the model, costs were between $17,990 for a Rancher to $25,990 for a Country Clubber. Before Strathmore, the township's population was centered in the Cliffwood section. Along with houses, Levitt built the roads and sewers, Strathmore Elementary School, Strathmore Bath and Tennis Club, and the Strathmore Shopping Center. He also deeded land for parks and playgrounds, property for churches, and a firehouse. Some original deeds for homes in the development prohibited picket fences and clotheslines. Even 40 years later, you don't see either from the street. Although Strathmore was the largest, it was not the only development. There was even some development in the borough with the building of 300 homes in the Marc Woods development.

The growth of the 1960s continued in the next decade, although at a slower pace with the Levitt and Sons Contempra development in the Freneau section of the borough in 1972. The development was promoted as only 38 miles from the city and less than an hour by train. The homes were described as bold in concept, imaginative in design, with a flair for elegant living. Contemporary lines of cathedral ceilings and wide vistas of glass were other attractions of the homes, as were the modern amenities of air conditioning, combination range-oven, refrigerator-freezer, and washer and dryer included in the price.

The population growth and construction of the 1960s came in more than just housing developments. The sheds and century-old former store of the Cartan and Devlin lumber and coal yard on lower Main Street were torn down to make way for 56 garden apartments. Contemporary with the development of Strathmore was a garden apartment complex, Aberdeen East. The all-electric apartments lost some of their luster a couple of decades later when electric prices sky-rocketed due to fuel shortages and inflation. In the mid-1960s, Tree Haven Village on Ravine Drive and the Balmoral Arms apartments on Aberdeen Road were also built.

A number of other significant events occurred between 1960 and 1979. Matawan Township Hose and Chemical Company built a new firehouse in 1968 at the corner of Lloyd Road and Church Street. Groundbreaking ceremonies were held during the summer of 1969 for the $1.5-million Matawan Mall Shopping Center at Lloyd Road and Route 34. The major anchor tenant was the W.T. Grant Company. Later tenants of the store were Nicols and Jamesway. In the late 1990s, the store became vacant and stayed that way for several years.

Much of the intimacy that used to be part of a small town changed with the increase of population. According to one local resident, "Before Strathmore, as

Church Street was a dirt road in this 1919 picture. Although the old farmhouse at 171 Church Street still stands, hidden behind trees, it was joined by hundreds of others as the farm fields became the Strathmore development. (Courtesy of Marie Dietrich Busch.)

129

a rule, everyone in the town knew everyone else. There were no K-Marts or shopping centers in the area. Everyone came downtown to do their shopping or banking." It was also mentioned that back before the days of shopping centers and central air conditioning, many people used to sit on their porches in the evenings. It was a common practice to sit and visit with friends or join neighbors on their porches. As you walked around town, you would greet the people on the porches or walking, even if you didn't stop. Even if you didn't know someone by name, you recognized them.

With the development of Strathmore and its accompanying influx of residents to the township, several new religious communities were created, including three synagogues. Illustrating how the communities of Matawan and Aberdeen have changed since the 1960s, the 1993 Community Thanksgiving Service was being held in the sanctuary of the Kimisis Tis Theotokou Greek Orthodox Church in Holmdel with Rabbi Weiner from one of the synagogues in Aberdeen speaking. For most of the existence of the area, neither of these two congregations existed.

Although the Keyport Jewish community from the turn of the century until World War II never numbered more than 60 families, there was an active synagogue life, drawing from Matawan as well as other Bayshore towns. The Jewish population of Matawan in 1936, as reported by H.S. Linfield in "Jewish Communities in the United States," was 25. That number would swell in the 1960s. In the northern part of the county, the Levitt and Sons Strathmore development added about 1,900 homes to Aberdeen Township tax roles in the early 1960s. The population grew from 7,359 in 1960 to 17,235 in 1980. According to statistics in *Peddler to Suburbanite*, "Approximately 30 percent of the new settlers [Strathmore residents] were Jewish." Within a few years of moving in, these pioneering Jewish families were instrumental in establishing two synagogues in the township. A third would come into being in the mid-1970s. By 1979, Aberdeen Township had three of the 26 Jewish congregations in the county.

In the fall of 1962, a small group of families, gathering at the home of Si Allweiss, organized the Strathmore-At-Matawan Jewish Center. The center was to become Temple Beth Ahm, a conservative congregation. The congregation first met in various public buildings around the township, including the Cliffwood First Aid Squad Building, Oak Shades Fire House, the Broad Street School, and later at the Matawan Township First Aid Squad's location, with members of the congregation or guest rabbis leading the services. Each fall, High Holy Day services were held under a huge tent erected at Church Street and Lloyd Road. Early Hebrew school classes were held in the Strathmore Elementary School and October 1964 saw 50 people enrolled in the school. The fall 1968 season would see over 300 people enrolled. Morris L. Rubinstein was engaged as the first permanent rabbi in 1964 and the congregation changed its name to Temple Beth Ahm, "House of the People" in Hebrew. After a decision was made to build a temple on the Lloyd Road site, an all-out effort to raise funds resulted in $201,000 pledged in an eight-week campaign. Construction of a synagogue was begun in 1967 and it was dedicated the following year. In March 1975, the nearly 100-year-

Much of the intimacy that was part of a small town disappeared in the 1960s. Residents such as Edith Johnson (left), seen posing in the backyard of Cherry Hall at 211 Main Street in 1897 with her niece, would have shopped at the (Commercial Block) store of William Gravatt Bedle (right) rather than a strip mall on the highway. (Bedle photo courtesy of Garrett and Mary McKeen.)

old United Hebrew Congregation of nearby Keyport merged with Temple Beth Ahm. In 1980, the Temple Beth Ahm congregation had close to 400 families.

In June 1963, a public meeting was held from which Temple Shalom—a new reform congregation to serve Matawan Township, Matawan Borough, and surrounding communities—would be formed. Part-time rabbis were engaged until 1965 when Rabbi Sheldon Gordon became the congregation's first full-time leader. Significant changes were to come to the congregation between 1968 and 1969, even though it was only five years old. The congregation had experienced such rapid growth that the original facilities were no longer sufficient for its 285 families and more than 400 students enrolled in the religious school. A new wing was added to the temple, providing office space, a gallery extension, and a 1,200-square-foot room, which served as a youth lounge or social hall when the folding wall was opened, or as two classrooms when closed. It was also during this time that a Czechoslovakian Torah was presented to the temple. The Torah had been found 20 years after being buried to save it from the Nazis. In 1980, Temple Shalom had almost 600 families.

Another congregation that came into the area as a result of the Strathmore development was the Cross of Glory Lutheran Church. According to the history of the congregation, Reverend Richard Weeden began working in the Matawan-Marlboro area to form a new congregation in June 1963. The congregation's first service was held on September 8, 1963 at the Strathmore Elementary School. The official Charter Sunday was held that November and the congregation incorporated the following April. Originally, the church was to be located on Route 79 and Orchard Parkway in Marlboro Township, but in the spring of 1965, the congregation accepted the first of two parcels offered by Levitt for religious purposes, and a sanctuary was built the following year. The congregation had a membership of 398 people when the sanctuary was dedicated in February 1967.

The Basilian Fathers of Mariapoch acquired 40 acres just off Monastery Lane in the township in the early 1960s for a monastery. When the Basilians moved in, the monastery consisted of a 100-year-old farmhouse and a chapel that was housed in an old machine shop on the property. Later, a modern building—with offices and a gold-domed chapel—and the Assumption Center with a 300,000-square-foot hall used for pilgrimages and retreats was erected on the site. The monastery serves as home to priests belonging to the Catholic Byzantine rite monastic order started in the fourth century. The Aberdeen monastery is one of ten Basilian monasteries in North America and is named in honor of Our Lady of Mariapoch, denoting its Hungarian roots.

Although located just over the border in neighboring Keyport, St. Joseph's Roman Catholic Church can be considered the first Catholic church for Matawan

Cross of Glory Church, at 95 Cambridge Drive, was rebuilt after the 1997 fire. (Courtesy of Cross of Glory Lutheran Church.)

residents. St. Joseph's was established in 1854, although the Reverend Patrick McCarthy, a circuit rider out of Perth Amboy, was preaching to area Catholics as early as 1850. With the influx of new people, the borough and township were to get their own parish when St. Clement's was founded on June 3, 1965. Reverend Joseph S. Rucinski was appointed the congregation's first pastor. Compared to the sanctuary of St. Clement's, the St. Joseph's 1879 red brick sanctuary where Matawan residents used to worship was small, only 30 feet wide and 40 feet long. Many local children still attend St. Joseph's school.

The first public Mass of St. Clement's parish took place in the auditorium of the Broad Street Matawan School at 8 a.m. on Sunday, June 15, 1965. There were two other masses that day, one at 10 a.m. and the other at noon. In less than a year, due to membership growth and the large number of children attending Sunday school classes, the number of Sunday morning Masses was up to four. Within six months of its founding, the parish had purchased and renovated the Demery home on Orchard Parkway in Morganville, New Jersey as a rectory and chapel for weekday masses and for confessions on Saturdays. The first baptism of St. Clement's parish, that of Michael Gregory Bliss, son of Joseph E. and Carol Wallace Bliss, took place in the rectory chapel on August 15, 1965. The first wedding, on October 31, 1965, united Chris Heuser and Marjorie Costello. In the spring of 1965, the congregation closed on a 22-acre tract known as the Crane property with frontages on Route 79, Ryers Lane, and Texas Road. A single-story, mansard roof, 800-seat capacity Catechetical Parish Center and Auditorium opened for services in the fall of 1970.

The formation of Calvary Baptist Church began in 1967 when Jessee Dilday, a member of the Monmouth Baptist Church in Eatontown, lead a small Bible study group in members' Strathmore homes. Within a year, the fledgling congregation was constituted as a church and property was purchased on Lloyd Road and Church Street. Meetings were then held in the house on the property next to the current church. Later, the house was used for Sunday school. In 1969, the congregation achieved another milestone when Jon S. Meek Jr. was appointed its first full-time pastor. The next significant landmark in the congregation's development came in 1977, when Pastor Elmer Vogelsang became the congregation's leader. Under Vogelsang's leadership, through the auspices of Builders for Christ, a church building was erected. Giving up two weeks of their vacation, 81 members of the First Baptist Church of Columbus, Mississippi came to New Jersey. Before they left, with the help of the Matawan-Aberdeen community and congregation members, a new church building had been erected.

A group of 13 families decided in 1975 that there was a need for an orthodox synagogue in the Matawan-Aberdeen-Hazlet area. Meeting in Daniel Lifschitz's home, they formed a new congregation, Bet Tefilah. Lifschitz's son, Rabbi Efrem Lifschitz, acted as spiritual leader as the slowly growing congregation held services in members' homes or in the South Matawan First Aid Squad building until the congregation built a synagogue on Lloyd Road in the summer of 1978.

With the population increase of the 1960s, area Catholics obtained their own parish. When St. Clement's was built, they no longer had to go to neighboring Keyport to practice their faith. (Courtesy of St. Clement's Roman Catholic Church.)

Effects of the population change in the township went beyond the township's boundaries. It also impacted on the residents and life within the borough. A typical example is that of the Methodist Church in Matawan. Although the church building at that time was still in the borough, the congregation, whose number of members had changed only moderately for many years, had a membership increase of 17 percent in a period of only four years. Other congregations in the town had similar effects as new families to the area sought houses of worship. However, the population changes did not benefit every congregation. Due to declining membership, the Cliffwood Community Methodist Church became a satellite of other congregations until 1981 when the congregation lost its charter and vacated the building. It was sold later that year and would eventually become the home of another congregation.

There were to be other traumatic changes in store for local Methodists. On August 26, 1965, the Matawan congregation voted to purchase approximately 8 acres on the corner of Atlantic Avenue and Church Street for $50,000. There were two main reasons why the decision to purchase the land was traumatic to the congregation: the cost and breaking away from the town. Unlike prior building decisions—like the one to build a church on Main Street, which had been more universally accepted among the members—the amount of money to build the new church on Atlantic Avenue (in excess of $100,000) was not acceptable to some members of the congregation. Another possibly more important reason was that after almost 100 years in the same building in the center of town, the church was moving not only off Main Street, but out of the borough to what is now Aberdeen Township.

The image of the red brick church in front one driving up Ravine Drive still remains a treasured memory to many old-time residents of the town. On June 21, 1970, the last service was held in the 116-year-old church on Main Street. During the summer, interim services were held at Temple Shalom, while the Atlantic Avenue church was completed. On August 30, 1970, the first service was held in the new Methodist Church on Atlantic Avenue, with cornerstone-laying ceremonies being held a few weeks later. The Main Street church was torn down and the lot was sold to Matawan Drugs for $40,000. The Church House was sold to the Farmers and Merchants Bank for $50,000. After being used by the YMCA for several years, it was eventually torn down and is now the site of the parking lot and addition for the Matawan Post Office. With the arrival of Reverend Robert H. Heulitt, the Methodist congregation was to experience one more significant change. The congregation received a pastor who would serve the congregation for 17 years, setting a length of time-in-service record.

The practice of exchanging pulpits and cooperative services between the various congregations in town has been going on since the 1800s. A forerunner of today's

The Calvary Baptist Church building was erected in two weeks as part of a cooperative effort between the community, the congregation, and the First Baptist Church of Columbus, Mississippi. This image shows people building Calvary Baptist Church, at 491 Lloyd Road, in the 1970s. (Courtesy of Calvary Baptist Church.)

The historic Methodist Episcopal Church was torn down in 1971 because it no longer met structural and usage requirements. Legal action was expected to take over the property for Post Office expansion. After more than 100 years, the congregation stayed in the area, but left the borough for the township.

community Thanksgiving service was held in October 1881. The Baptist and Methodist churches closed their doors so their members could participate in a Union Service that was held at the Presbyterian Church. The donations received during the service were to be used to aid the Howard Mission in New York, "a home for little wanderers." During the week of January 6–14, 1918, the other churches in town closed their doors as their members participated in a united churches revival campaign. One year, a joint Memorial Day service was held at the Methodist Episcopal Church with the pastors from the Baptist, Presbyterian, and Methodist churches officiating. Veterans rallied at the American Legion Hall and marched to the service.

One of the most noticeable effects of the dramatic increase in population was on the school district. The Matawan Regional High School on Atlantic Avenue was built in 1962. In addition to the basic courses, the high school offered a specialized vocational program, one of only three such programs in the county. The Strathmore Elementary School opened the following February to be followed by the Ravine Drive Elementary in February 1966. The Matawan Avenue Middle School and Cambridge Park School both opened in September 1970.

The Matawan school district was always, in essence, a regional school district and remained so even when the borough and township separated, thus setting the stage for it to become, in 1961, the first regional school district in the state under the new regionalization statute. A result of the change in the district's classification was a change in how the people were elected to the Board of Education with members apportioned between the township and borough. An 1874 letter to the editor of *The Matawan Journal* contained a paragraph that read, "still, they really should not allow a populous district to outvote less populous ones and deprive them of their rights: that is, by consolidating the schools." Even 40 years after the regionalization, some local residents still echo the feelings of the nineteenth-century letter writer.

The Matawan-Aberdeen Public Library of 2001 is a far cry from the first public library in the borough. Located at 165 Main Street, the current library has computers, public Internet access, and an automated circulation system. The first public library in Matawan, which dates back to 1861, contained 387 volumes and was located in the Collegiate Institute of Middletown Point. At the time, many churches also maintained libraries for use by their congregations. The library entered the twenty-first century with 82,484 volumes.

Founded in 1869, the Matawan Literary Society had a collection of 500 volumes housed in the dental office of Dr. J.P. Geran, located over Spader's Hall on Main Street, and later in the basement of society president William V. Simpson. The Glenwood Institute and Matawan Literary Society collections were combined with nearly 3,000 books donated by B.F.S. Brown to form the nucleus of a town library. Space was rented in a store in the commercial block for $1 per year and, in 1901, a reading room was opened for the town's residents. The following year, the Matawan Free Public Library was organized and officially opened its doors to

Courses taken by students attending the public schools in the 1960s were vastly different than those of students attending Mt. Pleasant School in the late 1800s, as advanced sciences and computer technologies have been added to the basic reading, writing, and arithmetic.

The white cottage on the corner of Main Street and Park Avenue, known as "The Smock House," served as the town library for 45 years until being torn down in 1966 for a more modern facility.

the public on October 1903 in the express office with Miss Edith Johnson as the first librarian. The number of volumes substantially increased over the next few years and over 3,600 volumes had been acquired by 1909.

When the property was sold in 1918, the library moved to temporary quarters in the store next to the post office. Shortly thereafter, work began on obtaining a permanent home for the library. Before that could be accomplished, after only two years, the library had to move again, as Anthony Rapolla tore down the building, and the library was without a home. That first permanent home was the little white cottage on the corner of Main Street and Park Avenue known as the Smock House. The site was bought in 1921 for $4,850. Originally a private residence for Garret Conover, the little cottage was built in 1830. With its rough-hewn timbers, Dutch divided doors, and wooden pegs, the cottage served as the library until 1966 when it was torn down and a single-story brick structure erected. Five years later, the J. Mabel Brown Children's Room was added. A two-story addition was completed in 1985. The store that had also been on the property was sold in 1927 to Forman R. Thompson, who moved it to Little Street.

In 1934, an informal arrangement was made with the township to support the library with the township appropriating $420 for the library budget. This informal arrangement continued until 1963 when voters of the township and borough formalized the Matawan Joint Free Public Library, which became the second joint library in New Jersey. The library would later change its name to reflect the township's name change.

While some businesses, such as the Vogue 4-Hour Cleaners at 131 Main Street, Feigenson Shoes at 137 Main Street, and Sandford's Pharmacy at 128 Main Street, advertised in the local papers during the 1960s and 1970s, most are no longer in existence; others from the same time period, such as Strathmore Lanes and Harris Hardware, have survived into the new millennium.

In the early 1970s, the Herricks decided to sell the Burrowes Mansion for restoration as a historical museum. On September 29, 1972, it was registered in Washington, D.C. on the National Register of Historic Places. The borough purchased the building on April 4, 1974. It has since been restored with one exception. It has remained white as was stipulated in the sale agreement. Koegler reported in *The Burrowes Mansion of Matawan, New Jersey* that the reason for the color restriction was that, according to Mildred Herrick, "I just don't like yellow. They paint a lot of old houses yellow and I like white." She continued living in the house until her death in the early 1980s.

In the fall of 1974, Reverend Lewis W. Kisenwether joined the First Baptist congregation as its pastor, and was still there as the congregation greeted the new millennium. The congregation also purchased the former Presbyterian manse next to the church at 234 Main Street. It was used for offices and Sunday school rooms until it was demolished in 1980 to make room for a new modular Sunday school chapel building.

Before automatic signal gates were installed, gatemen manually raised and lowered the gates on both Main Street and Atlantic Avenue. In between trains, the gatemen took shelter in their small shanties. The Main Street octagonal shanty was rescued and is undergoing restoration on the grounds of the Burrowes Mansion Museum by the Matawan Historical Society. (Courtesy Tom Gallo collection.)

8. To the New Millennium

In the 1980s, local residents watched football for more than seeing the Pittsburgh Steelers defeat the Los Angeles Rams to win Super Bowl XIV. They also tuned in to see local grid stars such as Jeff Shaw, Fedel Underwood, and Jim Jeffcoat, all of whom went on to play college or professional football. Jeffcoat, who was All American at Arizona State University, was a first round draft choice by the Dallas Cowboys in the 1983 National Football League draft. Shaw was a 1986 tenth round draft choice of the Cincinnati Bengals.

There were other happenings during this time. Some occurred as a result of local actions, while others had an international cause. Local men again went to war in early 1991 as American war planes in cooperation with a worldwide coalition of allies began striking targets in Iraq as part of the Persian Gulf War. Ground forces moved into Kuwait as part of Operation Desert Storm to liberate that country from the invading Iraqi forces.

There were also changes in some local religious communities. Although the discussions were at times heated, the Methodist congregation voted in 1989 to change its name. There were feelings that Aberdeen, the township the church structure now resided in, should be included in the name. There was also the feeling that Matawan, with over 150 years of heritage, should be retained in the name. The decision was finally made to change the name to the Matawan United Methodist Church at Aberdeen, which the congregation maintains as of the publishing of this history.

Founded in New York City in 1961, the Oversea Chinese Mission Church is a non-denominational Christian church with an emphasis on the support of missionaries overseas. The Jireh parish was organized in 1988 and came to Matawan that same year. The OCM-Jireh congregation met in the First Presbyterian Church on Route 34 and later in the Matawan United Methodist Church in Aberdeen. Illustrating how times have changed in the past 100 years, Trinity Episcopal, Matawan United Methodist at Aberdeen, and Cross of Glory Lutheran all had women ministers in the early 1990s—a situation that would have been unheard of in 1890.

The 1990s could be called the "decade of litigation" with the area gaining national prominence due to several high profile legal cases of national and

During his over 15-year professional football playing career with the Dallas Cowboys and the Buffalo Bills, Matawan Regional High School graduate Jim Jeffcoat played in 227 games, including two Super Bowls. In 1998, he joined the coaching staff of the Cowboys. (Courtesy of the Topps Company, Inc.)

international interest. In the spring of 1999, a township resident launched an email virus named "Melissa." After admitting to planting the virus, he was sentenced at the New Jersey Superior Court on charges of interfering with public communications. Melissa, which operated as a gigantic, virtually unstoppable electronic chain letter, generated hundreds of millions of emails a day, clogging systems worldwide and causing entire computer networks to seize up. It was later estimated that 70 percent of America's top 500 companies were hit.

The scouting organizations, the Boy Scouts and Girl Scouts of America, are one of the largest organizations in the world for youth of various ages. Over the years, both organizations have been part of the social and civic life of Matawan and Aberdeen as church congregations or other organizations sponsored troops of various levels. Sponsored at various times by Matawan's First Presbyterian and United Methodist congregations, Troop 73 of the Boy Scouts of America was at the heart of a precedence-setting lawsuit that went up to the United States Supreme Court. James Dale, an eagle scout who became assistant scoutmaster after turning 18, was for a time one of Troop 73's adult leaders. In 1990, the Boy Scouts of America revoked Dale's registration as an adult leader after learning he was gay. Dale sued the BSA in 1992, just after New Jersey's anti-discrimination law was expanded to protect the civil rights of homosexuals. In a 5 to 4 split, a divided U.S. Supreme Court ruled in 2000 that the Boy Scouts of America have the constitutional right to block gays from becoming troop leaders and that the

This residence on Cliffwood Avenue was torn down in the 1980s. Note the hotel (now Bruno's) barns in the background. (Courtesy of Aberdeen Township Historical Commission.)

New Jersey Supreme Court, which had previously ruled in the matter, was wrong in forcing the Boy Scouts to accept James Dale as a leader. However, the case was more significant than just the fact that it reached to the top court of the land. As a result of the case, school and public officials across the country held discussions and public meetings to consider rules for access to public facilities and public funding of organizations, including the scouts.

Plant and business closings were topics of interest to local residents in the 1990s as several long-time businesses closed their doors for the last time. In late 1993, a landmark in the center of town, the Foodtown Supermarket, closed its doors for the last time. Within a few years, the Spirits Unlimited store, which had replaced Foodtown, also closed down, leaving space for another major change as another long-time local firm, Harris Hardware, expanded and moved across the street into the former Foodtown store. The supermarket had a long history. Originally started by Abraham Belafsky as the Bell Meat Company, Foodtown was a family business, passing from father to son over the years. Although the store became part of the Foodtown chain in 1951, it still remained a family business and local gathering place. After a 1965 fire destroyed the original Foodtown building, a 10,000-square-foot building was built the next year. The expanded and more modern building did not secure the business' future, and it closed due to increased competition, the trend to the larger 30,000-square-foot supermarkets, and labor costs. In the summer of 1988, the 82-year-old Dell's Meat Market on Main Street also closed. A few years later, Anchor Glass Container Corporation closed its Cliffwood plant, laying off over 300 workers.

Like the other periods of the area's history, the 1990s were not without some significant fires. In late November 1992, a fire damaged the Presbyterian Nursery School on Route 34 and the adjoining First Presbyterian Church. A fire in the early morning hours of August 15, 1997 destroyed the old sanctuary of Cross of Glory Lutheran Church, which had just been turned into a parish hall. Severe damage was also done to the offices, kitchen, fellowship hall, nursery, and all of the classrooms. Only the new sanctuary, which was protected by a firewall and fire door, remained undamaged. Adding to the difficulty of the task of rebuilding was the fact that the congregation's pastor-in-residence, Reverend Gary Costa, was new to the congregation and had just preached his first sermon two days before the fire. Nevertheless, the congregation rebuilt, and the fellowship hall and educational wing were rededicated in the fall of 1999.

Vacant for some time, much of the former South River Metals Company on Church Street was destroyed by fire in late 1993. The fire, which caused about $1 million worth of structural damage, was ruled an arson. It took 50 firefighters from Aberdeen, Cliffwood, Matawan, and Keyport 11 hours to extinguish the fire. A second fire occurred 15 months later. The 14-acre site has a long history of industrial use from the Matawan Steel and Iron Company and the Wickham Company in the 1900s, to Munning-Loeb Manufacturing Company in 1911, Hanson–Van Winkle–Munning in the late 1920s, and M&T Chemicals in the 1960s. South River Metals Company moved onto the site in July 1975, making

Created by local Keyport artist Grace Graupe-Pillard, the centerpiece of the new Aberdeen-Matawan station is a 14-foot by 12-foot by 5-foot sculpture, "Gateway to the Shore," which features figures in leisure activities against the backdrop of the Raritan Bay. She also created works for the City of Orange, New Jersey and stations in Jersey City and Hoboken. (Courtesy of Grace Graupe-Pillard.)

143

parts for radios and televisions before going out of business in 1986. The site was assessed at more than $1.4 million in the mid-1980s.

One of the last controversies between the borough and the township during the last two decades of the twentieth century focused on the railroad and New Jersey Transit's building of a new train station. Unlike the previous two stations, which were both located on the borough side of Atlantic Avenue, the new station would be built on the township side. Township officials and residents wanted the station's name changed to reflect the station's location in the township. Borough officials opposed the name change, desiring to have the station retain the name it had for over 100 years. In the end, New Jersey Transit renamed the station to reflect both the new location and the history by calling it the Aberdeen-Matawan station. With the highest ridership on the North Jersey Coast Line, the new 1,500-square-foot station has a ticket office, concession stand, and 650 feet of high-level platform.

The last controversy of the twentieth century was the destruction of the landmark 1923 high school building. It ceased being used as a high school in 1962, when the new one was built on Atlantic Avenue. The old building continued to be used as a grade school through the 1970s, then later as office space for the board of education. In 1991, the borough acquired the old high school building, along with the former Broad Street Elementary School next door, for $475,000. The latter was converted for use as a community center and borough hall, and the former, vacant for many years, was razed in late 2000 after an engineering report found it was in danger of collapse.

After being left vacant for several years, the old high school building was torn down in late summer 2000. (Courtesy of Councilwoman Sharon Roselli.)

9. People and Lore

Over the years, a number of famous—and infamous—people have had their roots in Matawan-Aberdeen. Perhaps the most infamous, most enduring local legend involves Captain William Kidd. Although Kidd sailed the Caribbean, he did make several trips up the Jersey coast and at least one trip to New York City after becoming a pirate in the late 1690s. Kidd had previously captained a packet ship that plied between New York and London, and was reputed to have had a house on Liberty Street in New York City. Local legend has it that after becoming a pirate, Kidd stopped and buried treasure between the mouths of Whale and Matawan Creeks. William S. Hornor wrote in 1922 about treasure hunts inspired by the "old and worthless tradition, and by the finding on Money Island of a number of 17th century Spanish coins." Money Island was described as lying just off Cliffwood Beach. Hornor also mentions that one of two large elm trees, once known as Captain Kidd's rangers, stood on the top of Fox Hill (now Rosehill Cemetery) and the other was on the shore near the mouth of Matawan Creek. Local lore had it that the trees were used as range markers to guide Captain Kidd in locating the burial place of his gold. Many years later, Morrisey & Walker, Inc. would use the legend of Captain Kidd in the promotion of their developments. Their office, in the shape of a ship, was a local landmark for many years.

Perhaps the Matawan resident about whom the most has been written is Philip Morin Freneau, the Poet of the Revolution. Freneau was born in 1752 in New York of French Huguenots. His mother Agnes Watson was the daughter of one of the original Mt. Pleasant lot holders. Freneau's father purchased an estate at Mt. Pleasant the year that Freneau was born and the family moved there the following year. Some accounts, including one edited by a descendent of Freneau, describe the estate as a 1,000-acre farm. However, no record of the actual size has been found. No picture of the house exists, possibly due to the ravages of the Revolutionary War and a disastrous 1818 fire that destroyed the Freneau home, some family documents and most of Freneau's pictures. Philip Freneau was to spend much of his life in Monmouth County. An area was later to be named after him, although the pronunciation is different.

Freneau was an educated person and was admitted at the age of 16 to Princeton, where his classmates included James Madison, Hugh Henry Brackenridge (who later became a judge), Aaron Burr, and Lighthorse Harry Lee. Madison is said to have been a frequent visitor to the Mt. Pleasant farm. While at Princeton, Freneau began to write serious poetry, but the satires and romantic words later changed to a patriotic vein as the clouds of the forthcoming revolution began to gather. Freneau's writing espoused the cause of liberty. Freneau's cousin was another prominent Revolutionary War figure, General John Morin Scott.

Supposedly frustrated with his fellow countrymen's slowness in severing ties with England, just prior to the start of the American Revolution, Freneau accepted an invitation to visit Jamaica. His Caribbean travels included a six-month visit as the guest of the governor of Bermuda. Freneau returned to America in July 1778, arriving just after the Battle of Monmouth. Although most of the information comes from a pension application made almost 50 years after the fact and there are some discrepancies, Freneau supposedly fought with more than just the pen and wit he became known for. A week after his return, he enlisted in Captain Barnes Smock's Company of the First Regiment of New Jersey Militia. While he remained on the muster rolls until May 1780, he didn't spend the entire time soldiering. A descendent commented that Philip was so kind-hearted that he always found an excuse to leave the farm during slaughter time; the servants always killed poultry for the dinner table out of Freneau's sight. This aspect of his character, coupled with his love of the sea, may explain why most of Freneau's military service was spent captaining a ship privateering against the British.

There is an endearing story related to Freneau's time in the militia. According to Jacob Axelrad in *Philip Freneau—Champion of Democracy*, Freneau was stationed as a "scout and guard along the shore" between South Amboy and Sandy Hook. To avoid boredom, Freneau took his dog Sancho along on patrol. Sancho was supposedly wounded by a British saber during a local skirmish, making him perhaps the first American patrol dog to be wounded in battle. However, it should be noted that Freneau himself said that he was "in no battles, but several sea fights," and depending on when he told the story, Freneau was also struck by a saber or received a bullet in his knee.

According to Mary S. Austin in *Philip Freneau: Poet of the Revolution*, Freneau had a ship built in the Philadelphia boatyards and named the ill-fated vessel *Aurora*. When launched in late May 1780, the *Aurora* caught a small enemy sloop laden with corn. However, the capture delayed the *Aurora*'s passage around the point out into the open waters. When finally underway, a British frigate, the *Iris*, "one of the swiftest ships on the American station," was sighted and the outgunned *Aurora* headed for shore. However, before the ship and crew could reach safety, it was overtaken, the crew captured, and the *Aurora* severely damaged. Freneau was imprisoned on the *Scorpion*, an old transport vessel in which the British troops had been brought to the city. After his release in July 1780, while recuperating at his Mt. Pleasant home, Freneau wrote one of his most famous poems, "The British Prison Ship."

After the war, Freneau continued his literary work and married Eleanor Forman, daughter of Samuel and Helen Denise Forman (cousin of Black David).

The monument marking Philip Freneau's gravesite and that of his mother, Agnes Watson, overlooks houses on what was once the family estate. This image shows the Freneau Monument on Poets Drive in 1935.

He first edited the *Daily Advertiser* in New York in 1791, then the *National Gazette* in Philadelphia. He was given a job as translating clerk in the State Department by then Secretary of State Thomas Jefferson. In 1795, while living at his Mt. Pleasant estate, he published the first Monmouth County newspaper. It was suspended a year later for lack of support. It was also at Mt. Pleasant that Freneau published the state's first almanac. Freneau returned from another session of traveling in 1809 to settle down at age 57 at Mt. Pleasant with his wife, four daughters, and slaves. Austin's biography notes that Freneau freed his slaves before New Jersey passed the manumission law. Freneau and his family moved to the Freehold area after the October 1818 fire destroyed his Mount Pleasant home. After the death of his brother-in-law, Freneau moved into the Forman homestead in Freehold and lived there until his death in 1832. A popular account of his death is described by Austin as follows: Freneau met with friends at the rooms of the circulating library in town (Freehold), and while walking home, a sudden snowstorm came up. Freneau fell, broke his hip, and died. Freneau was buried on his Mt. Pleasant estate.

Philip was not the only Freneau who achieved a prominent position. In *Philip Freneau: Poet of the Revolution*, Austin wrote about Freneau's brother Pierre, or Peter as he was usually called. Pierre moved to Charleston, South Carolina, described as "a favorite location of Huguenot refugees," and served as Secretary of State of South Carolina from 1788 to 1794.

William Halstead Sutphin (1887–1972), who served six terms in the House of Representatives and two as mayor of Matawan, was known locally as "Call Me Bill." He resigned as mayor to serve in the Army Air Service during World War I. After the war he returned to Matawan and won re-election in 1921. This truck promoted the 1934 Democratic nominees, including Sutphin.

Freneau was not the only writer to have ties to the Matawan-Aberdeen area. In more contemporary times, Catherine Scheader, who moved to the township in the mid-1960s, is an award-winning author of children's biographies. She has written biographies for children on Shirley Chisholm, Mary Cassat, and Lorraine Hansbury, the playwright who created the ground-breaking play "Raisin in the Sun." Glenn Ficarra, who grew up in Aberdeen and Holmdel, attended Matawan elementary schools, and graduated from St. John Vianney High School in Holmdel, achieved standing in another writing form—the silver screen. Ficarra and John Requa co-wrote the screenplay for the 2001 Warner Brothers movie *Cats and Dogs.* The pair also co-produced the film that starred Jeff Goldblum, Elizabeth Perkins, and the voices of Susan Sarandon, Alec Baldwin, and Charlton Heston. In the movie, Ficarra was the voice of Russian Kitty.

In the 1800s, Matawan had several native sons who achieved notoriety beyond the town limits. Local lawyer William Dayton was attorney for the Farmers and Merchants Bank. He later became successively a legislator, a judge of the state supreme court, a senator, the first vice-presidential nominee of the Republican Party (when newly formed in 1856), and the ambassador to France during the Civil War.

Matawan's most famous native son was Joseph Dorsett Bedle (1831–1894). His father was Thomas I. Bedle, a local merchant, and his mother was Hannah Dorsett. In addition to his mercantile interests, Thomas was also a justice of the peace for upwards of 25 years and a judge of the Court of Common Pleas for Monmouth County. Thomas Bedle was, in 1857, the first tax collector and Overseer of the Poor in Matawan Township. Hannah was descended from a family that was among the early settlers of the county. Joseph Bedle obtained his early educational training at the Middletown Point Academy in Matawan, then later studied law under William L. Dayton in 1848. Dayton had a law office in Matawan for a short time in 1830. After being admitted to the bar of New York State in the spring of 1852, Bedle returned to New Jersey and worked for a short time in Henry S. Little's Matawan office before being admitted to the New Jersey bar. Bedle was a justice on the New Jersey State Supreme Court before accepting the nomination for governor at the Democratic State Convention in 1874. He won the election and served as governor from 1875 until 1878. During his term of office, Bedle brought reforms by calling for home rule, broke up collection agencies operated by justices of the peace, and instigated the creation of district courts. Perhaps the event he is most noted for is his use of the National Guard to prevent the rioting and property damage that occurred elsewhere during the 1877 national railway strike.

It was during the latter part of the eighteenth century that the Fountain family, which was to become a prominent local family in town, came to the area. The first Fountain of note was the Reverend John Fountain. John and the children

Another of the restored homes in Matawan is the late 1800s Fountain House, home of one of the area's early and prominent families. This image of the Fountain House, at 201 Main Street, was taken in 2002.

149

that he and his wife Elizabeth had together were to be a major influence on the town of Middletown Point. After injuries in 1797 forced him to leave the itinerant ministry and seek a more stationary lifestyle, Fountain took up permanent residence in the area known as Jacksonville, which later became known as Cheesequake. He revived Methodist activities in the vicinity of Matawan by conducting preaching services and holding revival meetings in a community church building in Mt. Pleasant. He was so well known that he was often called upon to officiate at funerals and weddings and became known as the "marrying preacher." A record in his own handwriting for the period of 1797 to 1834 shows that Fountain performed 406 marriages and 300 funerals. Rose Hill Cemetery was established in 1858 on land purchased from James Fountain. Other family members instrumental in the development of the town were Asbury, William, and Charles A. Fountain. William was one of the 27 founding members of Washington Engine Fire Company; Charles was involved with the Glenwood Institute.

Another prominent family for most of the town's history and whose members achieved prominence outside the local area was the Little family. William Little and his brother Robert were born in County Cavan, Ireland. A local merchant, William Little was instrumental in bringing the railroad to Matawan, in forming the Farmers and Merchants Bank, and in founding (with three others) the Middletown Point Academy. Many of the boys who attended the Academy boarded with the Little family. *The Matawan Journal* reported that when the Presbyterian Church, which Little and his wife Deborah Scott Little helped revive, was without a minister, "Little sent his horse to Princeton for the preacher who was to conduct the Sabbath services." One of their sons, Henry Stafford Little, was president of the Central New Jersey Railroad and president of the New Jersey State Senate. Among the dignitaries who came to town for his funeral in 1904 were former President Grover Cleveland and future President Woodrow Wilson, at the time president of Princeton University. One of William and Deborah's grandchildren was Henry S. Terhune, who was president of the Farmers and Merchants Bank of Matawan, and who became a justice of the state supreme court, as well as a member of the state senate through the Democratic Party.

There were also other famous descendents of Matawan residents. Lydia Holmes Bowne was an ancestor of President Abraham Lincoln. The Formans of the Old Hospital were the grandparents of Governor Horatio Seymour, governor of New York from 1853 to 1855 and 1863 to 1865. Seymour was also a presidential candidate, but was defeated by Ulysses Grant in the 1868 election. A great-grandson of the Burrowes and the Formans was Sidney Breese, a United States Senator.

Over the years, a number of artists and artisans have been associated with Aberdeen Township. One of the leading African-American Broadway stars of the 1950s, Juanita Long Hall, was born on November 6, 1901 in Keyport, New Jersey, and died on February 29, 1968 in Bayshore, New York, and was buried in Midway Green Cemetery on Reids Hill Road in Aberdeen Township. She enjoyed a long and varied career on stage, screen, and television. It was in *South Pacific*, the 1949 musical Pulitzer Prize-winning play, that Hall achieved her greatest fame as a singing actress. For her role as Bloody Mary, she received the prestigious Tony award. She went on to capture the role of Madame Tango in the 1954 musical *House of Flowers*, which was followed in 1958 with *Flower Drum Song*, where she played the principal role of Madame Liang.

One of the latest performers who at one time called Matawan or Aberdeen their home was Jodi Lyn O'Keefe. O'Keefe was born on October 10, 1978 and was raised in Cliffwood Beach. At the early age of eight, O'Keefe started modeling children's clothing for department stores. A graduate of St. John Vianney High School, O'Keefe's modeling experience led her to Los Angeles and an audition in 1995 for a part on the daytime television program "Another World," where she was cast at the age of 17 as Marguerite Cory, a role she held for approximately six months before leaving. Soon after departing the series, O'Keefe was cast as Cassidy Bridges on the CBS action drama "Nash Bridges," which starred Don Johnson and Cheech Marin. "Nash Bridges" premiered in March 1996 and ran until May 2001, before going into syndication. Among O'Keefe's film credits are "She's All That," "Whatever It Takes," and "The Crow: Salvation."

The 1960s were a time of cultural change as well as population growth. One local resident who characterized the changing times was Nancy Cromwell Woodhull. Woodhull spent part of her childhood in Matawan and graduated from Matawan Regional High School in 1963. As a pioneering journalist and feminist, Woodhull was sports editor for the *Detroit Free Press* in 1973 when few women even covered sports. Woodhull's professional credits included her roles as founding editor of *USA Today*, president of the Gannett News Service and of the National Women's Hall of Fame in Seneca Falls, New York, chairwoman of the Peabody Radio and Television awards, and vice chairwoman of the International Women's Media Foundation. She and feminist author Betty Friedan founded Women, Men and Media, an organization that monitored women's coverage, or lack of it, in the media. Woodhull died on April 1, 1997 at the age of 52 from lung cancer.

Woodhull was not Matawan's only pioneering journalist. Jeanne Mabel Brown, a descendent of Thomas Warne, was an important figure in the Matawan area, and as editor of *The Matawan Journal*, an influential one. After her father's death in 1920, Brown, known in town as J. Mabel, took over the newspaper, which she published until her retirement in 1971. Her civic contributions over the years were many; she was instrumental in the organization of the town's public library, founder of the Women's Club of Matawan, organizer of the Monmouth County Press Club, a charter member of the Bayshore Community Hospital board of trustees, and she became the first female member of the New Jersey Press Association in 1921. J. Mabel died on March 31, 1980 at the age of 94.

10. EPILOGUE

Some events like the 1941 attack on Pearl Harbor or the assassination of President John F. Kennedy become the defining moment of a generation. It is a moment in the generation when time stops for a second and everyone remembers where they were. September 11, 2001 was such a date and it has been said that a new generation of Americans lost their innocence that day. Although the suicide airplane bombings occurred in the twenty-first century, due to the effect on the town, which included the loss of more residents in one day than during the entire Vietnam War, no history of Matawan–Aberdeen would be complete without its inclusion.

Within minutes of each other, around 8 a.m. on September 11, American Airlines Flight 11 and United Airlines Flight 175 left Boston's Logan Airport with 266 people aboard on trans-continental flights to Los Angeles. Neither would make their original destination, and with a third plane that crashed into the Pentagon, would grab the attention of the world. A few minutes after takeoff, terrorists overwhelmed the flight attendants and crew and took over each of the jets. Flight 11 crashed into the 110-story north tower of the World Trade Center in lower Manhattan at 8:45 a.m.; shortly afterwards, Flight 175 crashed into the south tower. Although not as great an impact locally, a third hijacked plane that crashed into the Pentagon added to the tension of the day.

The crashes had a strong effect on area residents. The fire-softened metal of the World Trade Center towers gave way, and first the south tower and then the north tower collapsed. Thousands of workers, many from New Jersey, as well as the police and firefighters who had arrived to help evacuate the complex, were trapped in the millions of tons of rubble as enormous plumes of gray smoke and debris poured through packed narrow streets rimmed by Manhattan's enormous skyscrapers.

Later that day, weakened by the shock of the two towers' collapse, a third, smaller tower of the complex also collapsed in dust and flames. The total number of lives lost may always remain unknown. Two months after the attack, the unofficial count was over 4,700 confirmed dead or missing in the towers. By the first anniversary of the attack, the number of people confirmed killed had dropped to less than 3,000.

A temporary memorial built for the borough fire department's 2002 remembrance service in honor of 9-11 victims depicts the Pentagon, the World Trade Center towers, and Flight 93. It stood at Memorial Park on September 11, 2002.

What is probably the most significant effect on the communities of Matawan and Aberdeen is the number of people directly affected. Most of the New Jersey residents killed in the collapse of the World Trade Center were from Bergen, Hudson, and Monmouth Counties. Even local residents who were not directly affected knew someone who was killed or missing, or who narrowly escaped. Almost everyone in Matawan had some story to tell or knew someone who did. One local resident was working in Tower 2 and went outside after the plane struck Tower 1. As a result, he escaped without physical injury when the two towers collapsed, but was left trying to answer the question of why he survived when his coworkers did not. The psychological effects and the memories of the tragedies of September 11 are bound to linger for years in the hearts and minds of Matawan-Aberdeen residents.

At least eight residents from either the township or the borough were killed in the collapse of the towers. The number varies depending on whether mailing address or residence within the town boundary is the determining criterion. Among local residents killed were Steven P. Chucknick, Thomas A. Damaskinos, Virginia M. Jablonski, Robert Alan Miller, and Michael Uliano. Kenneth E. Tietjen and Richard Rodriguez, police officers for the Port Authority of New York and New Jersey, were also killed. Tietjen died when Tower 2 collapsed while he was helping rescue people trapped in the building. Another port authority employee,

The area has overcome many adversities, the most recent of which was the tragic events of September 11, 2001. The flag flying from the extended ladder of a fire department truck at the borough memorial service was just one of a sea of flags around town.

Stephen J. Fiorelli, was one of a group of about 16 people who initially stayed behind at the port authority offices to make sure the smoke situation was under control. People did not have to live in the borough or township for their loss to be felt. Some like Bernard Pietronico lived just outside the township boundaries. Others were former residents like Evan J. Baron and Lance Tumulty, captain of the 1987 Matawan High School football team. William E. Micciulli, Michael D'Esposito, and Marianne Simone had local ties through their membership in the congregation of St. Clement's.

Almost lost amidst the happenings in New York City and Washington, D.C. was a fourth plane, United Flight 93, that took off from Newark International Airport with 45 passengers and crew. Flight 93 was also hijacked. However, unlike the other flights, it did not crash into any landmark. The passengers on Flight 93 fought back to prevent their plane from being used as another airborne bomb, causing it to nose-dive into an empty field about 80 miles from Pittsburgh, Pennsylvania. The effect of the crash was directly felt by those in Matawan and Aberdeen as local resident Edward Felt was among those killed when the plane crashed.

The events of September 11 were personal in many ways to the residents of Matawan and Aberdeen. An almost eerie silence descended over the area as all air traffic across the country was stopped and the familiar sound of jets overhead suddenly ceased. The familiar noises of trains sounding their whistles as they crossed Main Street to enter the station ceased as New Jersey Transit stopped operations. Word of the events quickly spread around town. With television and radio coverage beginning just minutes after the first plane crashed into one of the World Trade Center towers, many local residents witnessed the events as they unfolded across the bay, either firsthand or on television. When the towers collapsed, television screens went blank as the major networks' broadcasting towers were destroyed. For several weeks, local residents had very limited broadcast channels as stations shared broadcast facilities.

The day after the crashes, Main Street in Matawan was a sea of red, white, and blue from one end to the other as a small American flag hung from every flagpole on both sides of the street. Flags of all sizes could be seen hanging from poles, tree limbs, and porch rails; in windows; and flying from car antennas. Flags too large to hang from poles were draped down the outside of buildings or strung across the front. Red, white, and blue bows and bunting adorned not only the stately homes on Main Street, but more modest ones on the side streets as well. Flags that covered the caskets of members of the greatest generation, a popular phrase for those who fought in World War II, were unfolded and draped across the fronts of homes. Other residents followed the words from a popular song of the 1970s and tied yellow ribbons on trees, porches, fences, and mailbox posts.

Although no longer the intimate environs of the early twentieth century where everyone knew his or her neighbor, residents of both the township and the borough responded to the tragedies of September 11. The borough held a memorial service in Terhune Park and the township held one in the high school. Among the fundraisers held for victims of 9/11 was a concert by noted erhu master Xu Ke sponsored by the OCM Jireh congregation. The recital was to benefit the families of Edward Felt and Neil Lai. Felt was a member of the Matawan United Methodist Church and Lai was a member of the Jireh congregation that met at the church.

Not all of the fundraisers were in support of local families; some helped to raise funds to benefit the families of other victims who lost their lives in the World Trade Center and to help out firefighters and their families. Members of the Aberdeen Hose and Chemical Company No. 1 raised $5,000 for Rescue Company No. 1 in Manhattan. Even the local children did their part to help the victims. The *Independent* reported that the students at Ravine Drive Elementary School held a "penny drive," collecting change in large water containers. The article also reported that the containers in the classrooms were nearly full after more than a week of collecting.

Although area residents have weathered the aftermath of significant events, such as Pearl Harbor and September 11, with the fast-paced lifestyle of the twenty-first century, unknown challenges remain to be faced and overcome. A quote in the spring of 1875 by *The Matawan Journal* editor David A. Bell is as true today as it was back then: "We are now on the verge of greater possibilities for Matawan [and Aberdeen] than have ever been known before."

BIBLIOGRAPHY

Austin, Mary S. *Philip Freneau—The Poet of the Revolution: A History of His Life and Times.* New York: A. Wessels Company, 1901.

Axelrad, Jacob. *Philip Freneau, Champion of Democracy.* Austin, TX: University of Texas Press, 1967.

Bradley, Barbara D. and Susanne D. Miller. *Matawan Memories: Word Pictures by Genevieve Donnell.* Matawan: Self-published, 1975.

Branin, M. Lelyn. *The Early Makers of Handcrafted Earthenware and Stoneware in Central and Southern New Jersey.* Rutherford, NJ: Farleigh-Dickinson University Press, 1988.

Church of St. Clement, Matawan New Jersey. South Hackensack, NJ: Custombook Inc., 1972.

Cook, Frederick J. *What Manner of Men: Forgotten Heroes of the American Revolution.* New York: William Morrow & Company, 1959.

Crosby, Alexander L., ed., Federal Writers Project. *Matawan 1686-1936.* Keyport, NJ: Brown Publishing and Printing Company, Inc., 1936.

Cunningham, John T. *Railroads in New Jersey: The Formative Years.* Andover, NJ: Afton Publishing Company, 1997.

Ellis, Franklin. *History of Monmouth County, New Jersey.* Philadelphia: R.T. Peck and Company, 1885.

Enterline, Stevenson and Trevor Kirkpatrick. "Index to Mt. Pleasant Cemetery—And Notations On The Presbyterian Church, Matawan, N.J." Manuscript. Matawan: Matawan Historical Society, 1989.

Fernicola, Richard G. *M.D. Twelve Days of Terror.* Guilford, CT: Lyons Press, 2001.

First Presbyterian Church, Matawan. *Presbyterians Pioneer at Matawan.* Matawan: First Presbyterian Church, 1959.

Gallagher, William B. *When Dinosaurs Roamed New Jersey.* New Brunswick, NJ: Rutgers University Press, 1997.

Gallo, Tom. *Henry Hudson Trail: Central Railroad of New Jersey's Seashore Branch.* Charleston, SC: Arcadia Publishing, 1999.

Gerlach, Larry R. *Prologue to Independence: New Jersey in the Coming of the American Revolution.* New Brunswick, NJ: Rutgers University Press, 1976.

Gordon, Thomas F. *Gazetteer of the State of New Jersey.* Trenton, NJ: Daniel Fenton,

1834. (Reprint, Cottonport, LA: Polyanthos, Inc., 1973)

Griffiths, Thomas S. *History of Baptists in New Jersey*. Hightstown, NJ: Barr Press Publishing Company, 1904.

Harris, Alexander. "History of the Methodist Episcopal Church, Matawan, N.J." Manuscript. Matawan, 1877.

———. "History of the Sabbath School of the Methodist Episcopal Church, Matawan, N.J." Manuscript, 1873.

Henderson, Helen B. "From the Back Street to Main Street: The Methodist Community of Middletown Point." Manuscript, Matawan: 1994.

———. *Around Matawan and Aberdeen*. Dover, NH: Arcadia Publishing, 1986.

Hodges, Graham R. *African Americans in Monmouth County During the Age of the American Revolution*. Lincroft, NJ: Monmouth County Park System, 1990.

Holmes, Frank R., ed. *History of Monmouth County, New Jersey 1664–1920*. Chicago: Lewis Historical Publishing Company, 1922.

Hornor, William S. *This Old Monmouth of Ours*. Freehold, NJ: Moreau Press, 1932.

Kennedy, Steele, Mabon et. al, ed. *The New Jersey Almanac: Tercentenary Edition, 1964–1965*. Trenton, NJ: New Jersey Almanac Inc., 1964.

King, David R. Jr. *The Episcopal Diocese of New Jersey, 1785–1985*. Diocesan Bicentennial Committee, 1985.

Kisenwether, Reverend Lewis W. Jr. *First Baptist in Matawan: A Constant Testimony*. Matawan: First Baptist Church of Matawan, 2000.

Koegler, Mary Lou. *The Burrowes Mansion of Matawan, New Jersey—And Notations on Monmouth County History*. Eatontown, NJ: Snell Graphics, 1978.

Kraft, Herbert C. *The Lenape: Archaeology, History, and Ethnography*. Newark, NJ: New Jersey Historical Society, 1986.

Lane, Wheaton J. *From Indian Trail to Iron Horse: Travel and Transportation in New Jersey 1620–1860*. Princeton, NJ: Princeton University Press, 1939.

League of Women Voters of Matawan, New Jersey. "Know Your Town: Matawan Borough and Township." Matawan: League of Women Voters of Matawan, 1965.

Lundin, Leonard. *Cockpit of the Revolution: The War for Independence in New Jersey*. Princeton, NJ: Princeton University Press, 1940.

Low, George C. *The Industrial Directory of New Jersey*. Camden, NJ: S. Chew and Sons Company, 1915.

Mandeville, Ernest W. *The Story of Middletown: The Oldest Settlement in New Jersey*. Middletown, NJ: Christ Church, 1927. (Jelliffe, Thelma K. Reprint. Middletown, NJ: Academy Press, 1972.)

Marsh, Philip M. *Philip Freneau, Poet and Journalist*. Minneapolis, MN: Dillow Press, 1968.

The Matawan Journal. Editions 1869 to 1973.

Miers, Earl Schenck. *Where the Raritan Flows*. New Brunswick, NJ: Rutgers University Press, 1964.

Monmouth County Directory for 1875. Freehold, NJ: J.H. Lant, 1875.

Morford, T.C. *Fifty Years Ago: A Brief History of the 29th Regiment New Jersey*

Volunteers in the Civil War. Hightstown, NJ: Longstreet House, 1990. (Reset text of 1912 edition.)

Moss, George H. Jr. *Steamboat to the Shore.* Locust, NJ: Jersey Close Press, 1966.

Nelson, William ed. *The New Jersey Coast in Three Centuries: History of the New Jersey Coast with Genealogical and Historic-Biographics Appendix.* New York: Lewis Publishing Company, 1902.

"Old Tennent Church." Old Tennent Sunday School. Tennent, NJ: 1957.

Pine, Dr. Alan S., Jean C. Hershenov, and Dr. Aaron H. Lefkowitz. *Peddler to Suburbanite: The History of The Jews of Monmouth County New Jersey from the Colonial Period to 1980.* Deal Park, NJ: Monmouth Jewish Community Council, 1981.

Reilly, H.V. Pat. *From the Balloon to the Moon.* Oradell, NJ: HV Publishers, 1992.

Reussille, Leon. *Steam Vessels Built In Old Monmouth 1841–1894.* Brick Township, NJ: J.I. Farley Printing Service Inc., 1975.

Richards, Horace G. *The Cretaceous Fossils of New Jersey.* Trenton, NJ: Dept. of Conservation and Economic Development, 1958.

Ryan, Dennis Patrick. "Six Towns: Continuity and Change in Revolutionary New Jersey, 1772–1792." Manuscript, New York University doctoral dissertation, 1974.

Steen, James. *New Aberdeen: or the Scotch Settlement of Monmouth County.* Matawan: Journal Steam Print, 1899.

Stillwell, Dr. John E. *Historical and Genealogical Miscellany Data Relating to the Settlement and Settlers of New York and New Jersey.* New York: Self-published, 1906.

Stephens, Jim. "From Our Correspondent With the 29th Regiment." Manuscript, 1999.

Tiemann, Mrs. Frank, ed. *Township of Matawan: 1857–1957.* Keyport, NJ: Matawan Township Centennial Celebration Committee, 1957.

Wardell, Charles H. Handwritten diaries, 1856–1918.

Wood, Don, Joel Rosenbaum, and Tom Gallo. *The Unique New York and Long Branch.* Earlton, NY: Audio-Visual Designs, 1985.

INDEX

Life in the suburban bedroom community that is Matawan Borough and Aberdeen Township of the new millennium is a far cry from the farms and orchards of the rural 1700s or the factories of the industrial 1800s. Firemen no longer need to hook their hose apparatus to the trolley to get to a fire, and the trolley itself no longer runs down Main Street. (Courtesy of Regina Hawn.)